Leader$hip
an insider guide

GIANNI ANCHOIS

ISBN:150844904X
ISBN-13:9781508449041

DEDICATION

This book is dedicated to my wonderful wife, son and daughter. Thank you for coping with me through the long hours I spend researching and writing my books, and for your unwavering support.

CONTENTS

LEADER$HIP - an insider guide

ACKNOWLEDGMENTS

I would like to thank Corrado Merlo, Michael Von Uechtritz, David Concordel and Stefano Burbui for being a steady source of inspiration, teaching and support throughout my professional life, first as colleagues and then as friends.
Special thanks to my friend Gianluigi "Gg" Redolfini for lending a hand when I was in need, and for endlessly providing wise tips and suggestions. To my readers, thank you for investing the time to read my book. If you enjoyed it, please take a moment to leave me a review at your favourite online retailer.

Gianni, January 2015

INTRODUCTION

What is leadership? How do you define a leader? Are leaders born or do they develop into leading roles? Do you need to be in a position of power to lead?

These are some of the questions that always fascinated me.

From a very early age, I've always been intrigued by larger than life historical figures, and eagerly read all the biographies I could find about them and their lives. As I matured over the years, I came to realise that most of those characters showed traits that could actually be distilled into attitudes, behaviours and actions that any of us could develop, nurture and perform.

Courage, determination, collaboration, honesty, values, vision, respect, trust, unselfishness are all signs of a good leader.

Although not everybody may want to be a leader, the potential is there for anybody to become one. Maybe not a leader with a capital "L" but certainly someone who can lead others by example, in public service as in private enterprises, and be the vehicle for them to develop into better professionals and ultimately better individuals.

Luckily, my professional life of over thirty years working for multi-national companies has provided plenty of opportunities for me to observe, learn, critique, shape, practice and codify practices and processes about the craft of leading people.

Having acquired a wealth of experience in areas like sales, marketing, business management and technology services, I found myself in the ideal position to analyse and interpret real-life leadership situations strongly connected to the world of business, and how to relate them back to an ideal blueprint.

The rich cultural diversity and variety of human relationship provided by working in multicultural environments, having lived in places as diverse as Europe, Latin America, Middle East and the United States, finally shaped my thoughts and findings.

This book is about those lessons learned. Here you will find reflections, examples and reference frameworks that will hopefully help you become a better leader, or will at least provide you with a number of lenses through which you can observe and better understand leadership.

I sincerely hope that you will enjoy my book.

1. THE BUSINESS OF BEING IN BUSINESS

Easy always beats hard. (M. Crichton)

Business is tough. You need to come up with products and services that are fulfilling a need. You have to figure out a way to build them. Then somehow you need to establish the best way to price, market and sell those products and services. You need to make sure anybody can and will buy them. You have to make sure you get the money. And finally you need to come up with more products and services.

The process can actually be fun, but somehow - especially for large established companies - most of the time it actually isn't.

SIZE. The process of starting and running a business doesn't really change that much with size. Two college dropouts working out of a two-car garage have to deal with the same problems of a multi-national enterprise with glass-enclosed offices in Manhattan. Small companies are nimbler, have a shorter line of command, can pivot quickly and can afford to fail fast (which is good in business). Large companies have established - and often cumbersome - processes that entail lots of checkpoints, reviews and approvals.

They are usually more resilient to failure - if they are well run - but when they do fail they fail big and hurt a larger proportion of employees, shareholders and clients. The headaches of both small and large are largely the same. How to develop products that fit the market. How to get clients to like them, buy them and then buy them again.

MARKETS. The definition of target market is mostly intriguing.

After so many years, I'm more and more convinced that all it is really is educated guesswork. The point is that market figures like market-share, share-of-wallet, growth and the likes are by definition projections. That means that someone by looking at the past behaviour of, let's say consumers, tries to map future ones.

Sure, big data and improved data analytics can help the accuracy of such exercise, but in the end the proportion of guesswork in even the most diligent market research is probably in the region of 50%. That obviously means that you have the same odds of being right than of being wrong.

PEOPLE. A third most interesting area impacting the life of a business venture is people. How many times have you heard statements like "our company values its employees as the most important and differentiating assets"? Well, guess what? They are right.

Employees should be the most important asset of any company. Truth is however that they are not really. When business is soft and the shareholders start to complain, the first motion is always to cut people. I've seen it happen so many times. The process is on average ruthless, although in same parts of the world where employees rely on stronger unions and better work contracts, it usually is kind of an acceptable way to go. Still, it never is painless. I still have to find a business leader who has the courage not to cut people when things are tough.

So how can anybody expect employees to be motivated when, no matter the role, experience or performance, they are always the first ones to get sacked? On the contrary, I believe that motivation is a driver that should come from within. I don't believe that a manager can motivate workers. He can certainly provide clear direction, chart the course and, most importantly purpose. The rest is up to you.

SO YOU WANT TO BE IN BUSINESS HUH?

You are determined that the next step in your professional life is to run a business. But do you have what it takes?

Here's a quick and dirty checklist that you can use to self-assess your readiness:

1. I know how my company makes money.
2. I know which clients are good (more profitable, less troublesome) for my business.
3. I know which clients are actually hurting my business.

4. I know how we build, market, sell, deliver our products and services.
5. I understand how to look for the best market opportunities.
6. I understand the dynamics of my selling costs.
7. I know how to articulate the innovation aspects of my products/services.
8. I have an engine in place to innovate my products/services.
9. I know which metrics are the right ones for my business
10. I measure the right metrics with the right tools at the right time.

If your answer is positive for each of the questions above, congratulations! You can now look confidently forward to running a simple business.

But what about a more complex one? How about a business unit in a company? Let's look at one of my favorite examples: the newly appointed Vice President.

How many times have you met executives holding important positions and carrying great responsibilities yet lacking the right skills for the job? That's right - quite often actually.

We are told that companies should "hire for fit, and train for skills", but actually it doesn't really happen that often, even less so for executive level hires or appointments.

In the current business environment, executives have to be fast and thorough at the same time, strategic and tactical, visionary and practical. I believe that, independently from the gravity of a given situation, any executive should and can set the mood early on in their management assignment. Yet it seems that a lot of them just act out the part, pay lip service or bide their time until they get the right opportunity and leave.

It's always hard to tell a VP what to do, I know.

Nevertheless, we can certainly tell them what we would do if we were one. As it often happens, good plans come in threes.

1. The first important piece to contribute is an aggressive 30-60-90 days change plan. Careful, not a shopping list! Rather, three to five key areas for each stage, to be reviewed, assessed and revamped.

2. The second important piece is to challenge everything you are told. Layers of middle managers are always ready to suck up to the new boss and fight for the privilege to whisper in his ear from selfish and often distorted perspectives. Even more so if the VP joins from outside the company ranks. Challenging is actually a very interesting and definitely underrated technique, I believe. For example, I'm deeply convinced that most clients, especially enterprise-class clients, know what they want, but not necessarily what they need. If you challenge your clients, and do your homework, you will be able to sell them what they need for the good of their business. And make a real difference. This very same approach of challenging the norm pays off quite well when dealing with internal "clients" too. And the reason is that if you challenge people, projects, activities often enough, you will make them

more effective. In turn, bright professionals never shy away from a good challenge, because they know that it's always, in itself, a learning experience. Checkout Eric Ries' "The Lean Startup" for an overview of the 5 why's technique of challenging assumptions.

3. The third and final piece a new VP should concentrate on is innovation. Over-innovation even. As Steve Jobs famously said "Innovation distinguishes between a leader and a follower".

Don't be afraid to introduce radical innovations in how things get done. Don't just setoff to modify a process, aim at simplifying it and re-writing it completely. Assess which parties are involved, focus their responsibilities and make sure everyone contributes to the final result. Make them clearly accountable. Give them a chance to make a real difference, don't treat them like gears in a bigger mechanism.

Streamline, simplify, ask your team to do less stuff, but to concentrate on the meaningful things. Don't make them work harder, set them up to work smarter. Be bold. Now that the three main rules have been applied, you are in a much better position to look at the most important element of your success – your team – and concentrate on your real job: to lead them.

Foster diversity: focus not on what is different, but rather harness the peculiarities of each team member to boost the team's creativity. Nurture passion: passion is how we engage, how we grow, how we move forward, how we keep going when everybody else in the race has given up. Passion is easy to spot in people, but it can just as easily be squashed if you, as a leader, don't show it too.

Understand what motivates people: what works for some team members might not work for others, so make sure you understand which is which. Give people purpose, and enough space to innovate and create, and they will feel motivated to perform great things.

There you go. Self-assess your business acumen and readiness. Make sure you have an aggressive change plan, challenge the norm and out-innovate your peers.

A PRACTICAL GUIDE TO BOOST GROWTH

I believe that more of the same never drives change. And without change, in most businesses and industries, you simply cannot achieve breakthrough growth.

A while ago, I was chosen as part of a selected group of people. The message we received requested us to make urgent arrangements for traveling to the south of France and plan to be away for a couple of days. The heading on the invitation only quoted the project name: "growth boosters".

The briefing that the small team was given was a simple one: to come up with ideas and a plan on how to drive breakthrough business growth. So we basically camped for two days in a medium sized meeting room, located in a remote off-site building, fully equipped with a couple of white boards, three flip charts, our laptops, plenty of food and soft drinks.

It's obviously difficult, and potentially tedious, to try and reconstruct that monster brainstorming session. However, I think there is value to share some of the outcomes: after all, the problem of driving business growth is still pretty high in priority for many of us!

First step was to look at dependencies for the success of our plan: who or what would be the biggest potential help to successfully implement it? We definitely needed to identify friends and foes early on, and secure sponsorship plus endorsement from the top.

Second step was to identify the key desired milestones:

- build a community focused on growth:
  - provide a strong sense of "why" we were embarking on growth boosting initiative ('what's in it for me?").
  - identify what was the passion behind it
  - articulate why we needed everybody on board
  - define the role that each of us would play
- share and celebrate progress and success:
  - tell the "good" stories and provide better visibility to key wins.
  - go beyond the congratulatory email or card and give "social" visibility to winners, at personal and team level.
- recognize excellence:
  - reward best deal of the month.
  - shoot promo videos.
  - give free vacation days.
  - reward individual and collective contribution with technology gadgets.
  - donate cash to favourite charity organization.

Pretty soon we realised that we needed to somehow package the whole effort into a sort of company-wide container, a powerful message or communication push to catch people's attention. We devised an internal marketing campaign across some low cost actions:

- PING – Personal Impact of Non-Growth: a semi-serious tool to assess the impact on one's career, development and earnings of non-growing the business.
- fit for growth boot camps: hands-on focus days for small teams, geographically or vertical industry oriented.
- music jingles and ringtones: branding exercise to distinguish top performers and create competitive tension.
- customized laptop sleeves: another branding exercise, to identify tech rewards to best achievers.
- T-shirts and promotional materials: fun stuff for the whole community to repeat and amplify through word of mouth.

Next we zoomed in on the specific working tools that we would need to develop to empower the growth teams:

- dedicated personal and team websites (i.e. mygrowth.com), wikis and forums.
- top management MBWA program (Management By Walking Around), to effectively turn our leaders into our stronger advocates.
- roadshow to be taken to the key European offices. This was developed as a play, complete with actors impersonating both clients and sales teams, going through

examples of sales situations and typical business engagements. The roadshow was also filmed and relayed on the intranet in instalments.

- a video game to simulate desired behaviour and interactions.

Finally, we toyed with funky ideas about how to motivate our large sales force, like putting up huge countdown (sales) quota indicators in the reception hall of our campus, setting up a phone hotline for depressed sales reps ("My client hates me, help!!!") or building a client's fanzine.

We also concentrated our efforts on how to improve our storytelling capabilities, something we didn't usually do very well. Coaching sessions with actors and comedians were taken into consideration, as well as the establishment of an internal TV channel for employees to practice one-to-many storytelling.

All in all, an incredibly fun project! In retrospect, with today's social media tools, we could have implemented some of the ideas above in a radically different way, certainly reaching out faster and better to our desired audience, and through a richer experience too. But I still believe that some of the things we developed and built were cool and are very much applicable today.

THE REAL MEANING OF GO-TO-MARKET

A lot of people misunderstand the real meaning of go-to-market. So here's a simple is/isn't list to remind us:

IT'S NOT
1. It's not about your product features.
2. It's not about your price.
3. It's not about your competitors.
4. It's not about your marketing plan.
5. It's not even about the so called "differentiators" of your offering.

IS
1. It's all about your clients and the best way to reach out for them.
2. It's about empowering your sales force to select the right clients and make the right recommendation about what works for them.
3. It's devising the best tactics to showcase "why you".
4. It's about understanding where the market will be, not only where it is.
5. It's about choosing the best places to hang out at (hint: where your clients are).

Now that I think of it, route-to-market makes a lot more sense, as a broad definition, than go-to-market. Think about the classic definition of a market. A place where manufacturers and sellers go to show and sell their stuff. And of course a place where people go to look at what's available (e.g. window shopping through the stalls) and possibly buy something.

So the common wisdom is that, assuming there is a market, people will go there. That's the easy part right? As a seller, you show up, hence you've gone to market. To do that doesn't require you understand it, size it or truly know it in any details. You trust the market: if you build something, somebody will buy it. Of course this is an oversimplification of market dynamics, and of course it doesn't really work like that anymore.

But what if you have to decide a route to the market? Then something different may happen. You will have to choose a path to get there. Short and quick will ensure you are first, maybe before your competitors but possibly even before the market is mature enough for your offerings. So, little or no buyers.

Long and arduous, may mean you will be second or third, potentially having to fight off an incumbent player, but also that you will have had a chance to learn from other's mistakes and maybe just think longer of the problems you are endeavouring to solve. And buyers might have more choices but be more self-aware of what they need.

Now, here's the big decision that you as a seller need to make: which route do you want to take?

Is your company targeting established, experienced and shrewd buyers/clients, or fairly new – and potentially unclear in requirements – ones? Let me tell you why I think this is important.

If you go for the experienced clients, your value proposition will need to stress areas like cost saving, efficiency improvement, risk aversion and in general status-quo protection.

If you choose the newcomers, than you will need to leverage the market disruptive elements of your offering. The bleeding-edge – but potentially unproven and risky – technical proposition that will empower the client to change the rules of the game and dislodge the incumbents from the playing field.

The decision about your route-to-market will make your offering more relevant to the market, and will enable you to articulate it in a way that resonates with your chosen audience. It will even make you look at the components of your offering in a different way, and feed back to your design team to adjust and align them to the chosen path.

So think of this next time you are building your business plan: do I need a go-to-market strategy, or should I chart the route-to-market for my offering and products?

MAKE SURE YOU ARE ALWAYS CREATING NEW IDEAS

When is the best time for you to come up with your best ideas? For me, it's when I'm in meetings and events!

When somebody is presenting or pitching to an audience, I always try to pay attention. My mind, however, pretty soon starts thinking about a million possibilities, and goes on a lateral (but not disjointed, as you will see) quest.

Just like many of us, my daily routine is to sit through a lot of presentations and pitches. Some are in person, but most are through phone conference calls, IM and other collaboration tools. Lately, I've come to realise an interesting pattern that I go through pretty much consistently and almost unwillingly.

As the speaker illustrates her materials and point of view, a portion of my brain starts on a journey of its own. Suddenly, whilst still paying full attention to what is said and shown, my mind start bringing up ideas, perspectives and original observations on a number of topics. Sometimes these are related, or at least tangential, to the ones discussed in the meeting; other times they are completely different, and apparently disconnected. The experience is interesting because connection and branching happens almost effortlessly, without any planning and certainly with no defined story boarding.

Especially at in-person presentations and events, this process can be very fulfilling if somewhat tiring, particularly because on top of listening and watching the speaker and his materials, I'm in the habit of scanning the audience for reactions, body signs, comments or remarks.

What I've found is that this practice fundamentally enhances the experience of the event and makes it more complete; by establishing a link between giver and receiver, one can take the whole exercise to a new level, where the two entities fulfil each other and at the same time keep each other in check.

A good and engaging presenter usually pushes your mind to expand on the things he says. In addition, if the material he uses is also good, you have a chance to imagine how a story could be crafted around it in a way that would bring its message even more relevantly to the audience without changing much of the content – a victory of form and context over content.

But, surprise surprise, for me the magic happens when the presenter and/or the materials are not particularly good.

Far from discrediting the effort of the speaker, when that happens my brain floods with tag-lines, words, visuals and a million ideas about how to improve the presentation, on a scale that is almost too big to take in. Often it's all about painting "what if" and "why not" scenarios, other times it's about digging deeper into a certain aspect and sketching out a whole different outcome.

The best way to capture this is to start jotting down short notes and hints, hoping to be able to recall the thought process at a later date, and maybe share some of the ideas back with the presenter and the audience. Try to imagine how the content being shared could be brought to life from different angles and perspectives. How things not being said are actually more important than the ones that are. And how what is presented as a minor detail, or sometimes left out altogether, should actually be positioned as the core reason why we do what we do.

Let the visuals jump at you and completely rework the ones on the screen, trying to reflect the new sentences and underlying message that your brain has just put forward. In my case, I often end up not sharing much of my mind's flight with anybody else, although I do tend to incorporate some of my best ideas into new projects and plans, certainly never providing full explanation of the true genesis of my insights (for some reasons, I discovered you can actually offend, and even hurt, people if you do).

Another intriguing fact is that all of the above can happen on topics completely different from the ones being discussed at the moment. So for example, a presentation on the latest technology for migrating IT applications to the cloud can trigger thoughts about the education system and how schools are using 19th century techniques to try and teach 21st century's students.

Best of all, those little impromptu brainstorming sessions with yourself can provide endless topics and ideas for future blog posts, articles, business initiatives and activities.

YOUR COMPANY MIGHT BE TOO BIG TO MATTER

Size is often mentioned as a key differentiator for enterprises. In boardrooms across the world, it is largely believed that size alone will make a company achieve economy of scale, and magically make it more competitive and hence successful. Whilst for certain specific industry segments this might technically be true - for example in mass production of consumer products - I think that for the large majority of companies size can actually be detrimental and play a key role against growth and success. Nimbleness, flexibility, adaptability are much better attributes, bigness is way overrated.

In my observations through the years, when a company becomes too big, a number of things happen:

1. decision making becomes cumbersome and slow: what happens is that there are simply too many reporting lines and approvals to be obtained, and processes to get those approvals usually suck. Back and forth endless threads of emails are usually a good indicator of this happening.
2. matrix organizations flourish: direct reports, dotted line reports, functional teams, local and global span of control. All effectively diluting and blurring the command line, and building a deadly fishing

net. Few - if any- employees will ever be able to escape.

3. less risk taking is accepted: the sheer size of needed approvals will take care of squashing any even moderate risk that your initiative might entail. Should that not be enough, the matrix organization setup will take care of killing any innovative out-of-the-box effort.

4. over-measurement and over-analysis: as the former HP CEO Mark Hurd used to say, "if you torture numbers hard enough, they will tell you the truth". Problem is, the truth is not necessarily what you want to know when you are trying something truly new. What you need is to be completely confident that your radical and innovative action will produce an impact, hopefully - but not necessarily - a measurable one.

5. take forever to launch products/services: a direct consequence of the matrix setup and cross-approval process, by the time your products/services are launched, the market has moved on (sounds familiar?). A sense of omnipotence takes over, making these companies think that they know better than the market. They almost never do.

6. a lot of lip service and sucking up: enough said.

7. micromanagement rules the floors: because huge companies are so paranoid, articulated and complex in nature, each one of the managers and supervisors becomes really averse to risk taking. The natural instinct therefore is to structure everything into templates, framework and strict processes,

sort of exponentially increasing the big-brother approach.

If you really want your company to have impact, I believe that it should:

- be nimble: trim down your processes, measure only what really matters.
- be quick: a product 80% ready is good enough, ship and keep improving based on the market and clients feedbacks.
- empower your employees: trust your employees to make decisions, try something new, fail often (as long as you learn from your failures). Encourage people to move out of their comfort zone, so they can acquire new skills and competencies.
- be on the market: listen to clients, know their business models and needs, do not impose your in-to-out point of view on them.
- be where your clients are: nourish the relationship with them (something very difficult to do when you are only talking to clients to make a sale...). It takes time, dedication and real interest in what they do and how they perform.

A huge company might achieve operational savings by consolidating and sharing some common functions – HR, invoicing, corporate marketing – but it will be unable to devise and rollout a real growth engine just because of scale and size. Also, it's really very difficult to achieve breakthrough and accelerate growth when you keep doing the same things over and over again. Cost control and happy shareholders can only take a company so far.

Instead, companies that are nimble, that empower workers, that allow and even endorse risk taking and failures, will be the ones that, by creating an innovative environment, will most likely than not achieve real significant growth.

PRACTICAL EXERCISE

You can use the checklist below (courtesy of the Harvard Business Review blog network) to map your current situation.

1. I fully understand and play to my strengths
2. I successfully leverage the talents of others
3. I effectively use my skills to serve others
4. I constantly look for new challenges and projects
5. I take intelligent risks that often take me out of my comfort zone
6. I constantly expand my professional network
7. I build trust through consistency and caring in my relationship
8. I maximize my positive effect with the minimum means
9. I constantly seek to gain or create new ideas and knowledge
10. I have clear and compelling goals that are in writing
11. I stay alert to emerging trends that can potentially affect my work and life.

12.I leverage times of adversity to reflect and redirect my energy.

WHY DO YOU SHOW UP AT WORK?

The alarm goes off. Time to get up and get another day started. You force your legs out of bed and lift your butt off the warm sheets. You shower and shave, gulp down your first cup of coffee and get dressed. Drive 20 minutes to the office and park in the usual spot under the old oak tree. You go through your day like a robot and at 5pm sharp get into your car and head back home. Does this sound familiar?

There are thousands that live their working life just as described above. No game-plan ahead. Auto-pilot. Cruise control. Monday morning cravings for the weekend to start.

Every day feels the same, an overpowering sense of wasted time and no way to stop it.

It's wise to assume that with the current economic climate and the high level of unemployment it brings, we should consider ourselves lucky to still have a job. Thousands of workers every day get their job engagement terminated, whilst at the same time youngsters find it harder than ever to find one. Companies seem to be ruling almost exclusively by fear.

However, if we try to get out of this "fear mode" for a moment (or if we ignore the lizard brain as Seth Godin calls it), are you sure you really know why you bother to show up in the morning? I know, you're thinking "Duh?! Because they pay me, so I'd better go to the office!" Sure, but really? How about actually bringing your brain to the office too? And since you are taking your brain for the ride, how about getting it ready to roll on the way to work?

I have observed how a lot - and I mean a lot! - of people who think that to be working means to show up in person. These are the ones that pretend to be there but are really somewhere else. You've seen them. The ones that passively go from phone call to phone call or from meeting to meeting without really adding or learning anything, much less getting anything valuable done. I call them sleep-workers.

There must be a way to counter their state of mind. A proven methodology to get the brain revved up for another day of hard and rewarding work. A system to guarantee not only physical presence at the cubicle, but actual readiness to purposeful contribution.

How about a little practical routine:

1. as you have your breakfast in the morning, or first cup of coffee or whatever else you usually have, mentally list the three things that you want to accomplish today. At least one should be work related.
2. as you shave, put your make up on or generally get yourself presentable, break down those three things into a few main actions. For example, let's say that you want to learn about a new software tool. The three actions could be: download a trial version, printout the quick user guide, test it. Set a timer for this, let's say 60 minutes and stick to it.
3. as you make your way to the office, think about three things that you do not

want to do today. For example, attending a boring review meeting, or joining the others in the canteen at lunch time. Stick to your proposition and just don't do it. Not doing stuff is more important than doing it.

4. Spend the first 15 minutes at your desk by putting into writing your thoughts as developed above, and get started.
5. At the end of the day, just before leaving for home, spend a few minutes ticking off any of the activities you planned for your day first thing in the morning.
6. Re-Do.

I've used a similar routine every morning for many years, and I found it very helpful. It's simple but it really gets me going, and it sharpens my brain and senses into getting to work with a positive and can-do attitude. Some days it comes easy, some others I find it very hard. But no matter what, if I miss my little routine even for one single day, I really don't feel right. Like athletes and sportsmen, repetition hones your skills.

Brains are just a very sophisticated muscle that happen to be so powerful to drive everything else in your body, including emotions, feeling and ultimate well being.

A word of warning: if you get into this proactive awakening behaviour, you will certainly improve the quality of your working days, but you will also notice even more how others behave like you used to.

(MARKET) SIZE IS IRRELEVANT

Consider this:

1. your company is large and healthy.
2. you are either #1 or #2 in each and every market segment where you play.
3. your revenues grow (moderately), your profit also (slightly) and your cash flow is positive (very strongly).
4. your R&D departments churns out new and exciting products on a regular basis
5. you have a large and largely loyal customer base

Now here's the question: is this the right time to stop worrying about what the market wants? Instead of chasing the impossible - i.e. building something that everybody believes they want - should you focus on building what you think the market will want and make sure you reach out to your customers and explain to them why they want it?

In other words, if you are the 800 pounds gorilla, you rule the forest. Just make sure your customers will keep trusting you and buying stuff from you, don't worry (too much at least) about changing requirements. Or not?

If you are not an established company however, you need to reconsider your game. Specifically for a newborn company, you'll be better off by talking about clients rather than markets.

More important than any business plan or even a minimum viable product (MVP), making sure you know who your clients are is what will get your company off the ground.

Decide as early as possible which client you want to delight with your products and services, and define what is the better way to reach out to them. Talk the language they talk and spend time where they do too.

How many clients you'll be targeting is still fairly irrelevant in terms of sheer size, especially because you don't want to dilute your limited resources or capabilities by trying to address a too big potential client audience.

If you focus your efforts on the right amount of clients, you'll be able to learn all there is to learn about them, and lead the discussion when engaging. If you are casting your net on a market/client base that is too wide, you will not be able to be relevant or innovative. Remember to be listening but also don't forget to provoke discussions. Keep in mind that it's good to provide what clients want, but also that many clients don't really know what they need.

To quote Steve Jobs again, "innovation is about providing something people did not know they wanted".

2. SALES SELL

The core principle of any business is to sell something.

Mostly in exchange for money (products, services, sometimes at no charge (ideas, page views, share of mind), but still the key act is to sell.

Now, before you embark on any business activity please make sure you understand the following key principle. If sales don't sell, fire them.

Let's be even clearer. Sales is a company function. As a company function, the purpose of sales is to sell. If sales don't sell, you have a problem. If your sales manager misses his quota two quarters in a row, you have a sales problem. If he misses four quarters in a row, he has got a job problem - in essence, he's out of one. Too often I've seen condescending sales directors and Vice Presidents get away with murder. The signal sent to the rest of the company is devastating.

Pretty much every sales organisation works alongside the following lines:

- The company has a portfolio of products (in case you wonder, yes - services are products these days).
- They are designed, engineered and manufactured, and need to be sold.
- The company functions assigned to selling the products or taking them to market are many: business development, tech support and, naturally, sales.

The process of selling is one deeply ingrained into human beings: we sell ideas, we sell principles, we sell attitudes. Our politicians mostly sell dreams they have no intentions of fulfilling.

Hi-tech products and services sales usually require a fairly complex process or sales cycle. Sales reps are assigned sales quotas. Sales managers build sales targets based on previous year/quarter performance, and staff their sales teams with account managers, sales execs, sales reps, specialists, generalists, etc. Mostly, sales teams keep doing the same things expecting different results. Guess what? They will fail.

Unless you modernise the sales process, and embrace the social and digital platforms to do so, you're going to fail big time. One of the key reasons for failing of course is that current buyers are very different from what they used to be.

Buyers today do a lot more research online, require a broader adoption of engagement tools and techniques, and often prefer to engage remotely. Social and digital marketing, based on a free-content available to all approach, have changed the way buyers learn about products and services.

Arguably, better informed potential buyers are actually tougher to sell to. Modern buyers also favour purchase decisions via the web, phone and social media, with no unnecessary face to face interaction unless it brings real additional value to their decision making process.

Hence you should re-design your sales process to take into account all of the above changes, and have a much better chance to sustain your sales expectations and ultimately drive business growth.

Additionally, you should also be looking to accelerate your sales practices, by leveraging client knowledge tools like big data analytics, as well as sales automation and marketing automation software. This will help you scale your efforts more efficiently, and at the same time provide a better sales experience to your increasingly demanding buyer.

Finally, you should not forget sales enablement. Across the sales process, sales reps need to know what content to present to which prospect. Nothing is more important than having relevant information for each and every client, and avoiding the one-fit-all approach.

Always remember that to show up is a solid start, but to show up with something relevant to your client and ready to be sold is a much better one!

PRECISION SELLS

Accuracy. Precision. Very often the two words are interchanged or even used as synonymous, but they actually have very different, specific, meanings. Why is this important for your sales team and the way they target customers?

It is safe to say that all sales plans are built starting with a key assumption: let's find the best prospects for our products/services. Best prospects are usually defined as "those clients that have a need, a compelling reason, a mean ($$) and an intention to buy now". Even better if your company does business with them already.

Typically, as you go and develop the sales plan itself, you look at funnel data, installed base population of clients, and at a lot of market data to identify an addressable market.

In a nutshell, you hope to predict the future by looking at the past – not a particularly easy thing to do. What most people do not often do, however, is to make a fundamental operational decision: are we going in for accuracy or for precision?

Quick look at the definitions first (source Wikipedia):

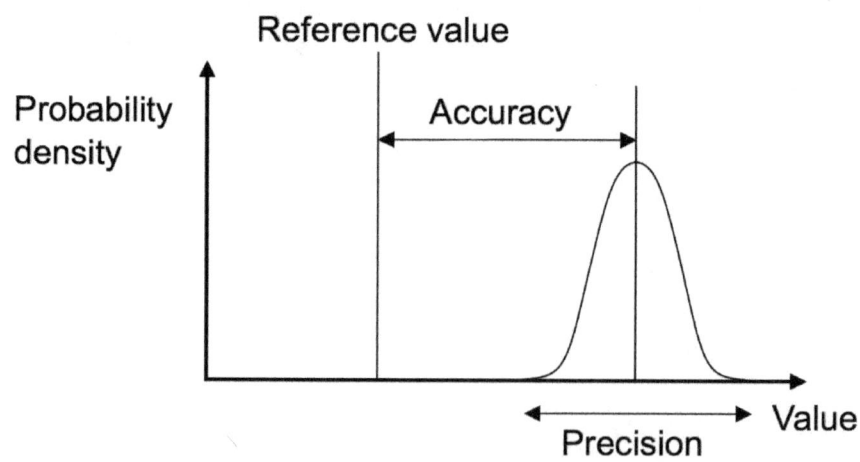

Accuracy: it's the degree of closeness to a standard value.
Precision: it's the degree of closeness of two or more measurements to each other.

Let's use some visuals to better understand what those definitions really mean:

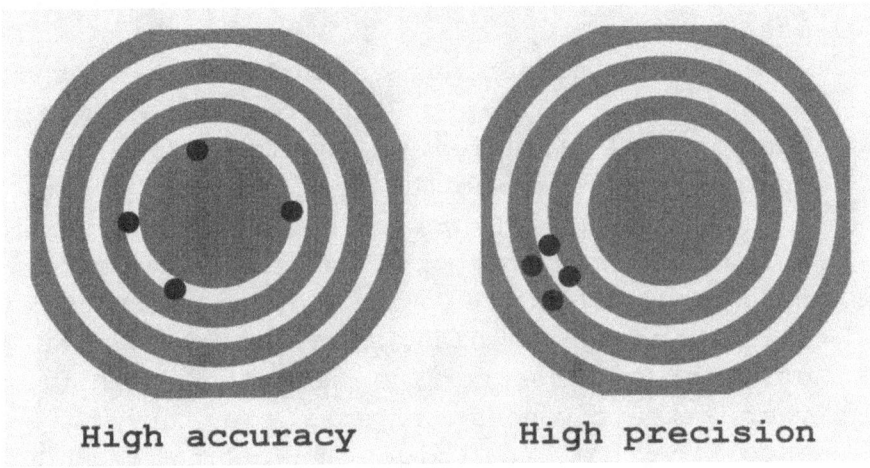

High accuracy   **High precision**

In other words, if your sales teams are accurate, they will shoot for the best fitting prospects: the bulls eye. They will quickly qualify out those clients not matching the established criteria, and possibly quite rapidly run out of potential buyers. This is not necessarily a bad thing to do, especially if you are selling to a niche market.

If your sales teams are precise, on the other hand, they will probably identify a cluster of prospects that, although not 100% fitting the criteria, will buy your products again and again. Once that specific cluster is exhausted, the sales teams will move on and identify another, probably adjacent to the previous one. This apparent "slack" in the application of the criteria, sort of a proxy approach, might require a longer sales cycle, or even a lower amount of per-client revenues, but those effects will likely be compensated by the consistency and repeatability of the sale.

Now here's the big question: as a sales manager, which of the two teams would you like to lead?

The obvious answer is that a mix of the two behaviours – accuracy and precision – would be the optimal solution. I would argue, however, that it would not be the best choice.

Personally, I would rather trade accuracy for precision. My point is that no matter how hard and diligent you are when building your sales campaign or plan, there is always the risk of being too restrictive with the definition of your attractiveness criteria. You try to be so specific that you might unwillingly shut out whole portions of your client base or addressable market even before you start selling. After all, how many bulls eyes are there in a target?

If you allow, instead, for less accuracy but encourage precision, you might discover new criteria you never thought of in the first place. Clients might actually scrape the money together to buy from you, for example, or they might like your services so much to be willing to revise their project's priorities. In some cases, clients would want something and be waiting for somebody – you and your team – to actually sell them what they need, instead. The periphery of the target is also, in absolute terms, way much larger than the bulls eye area, so a bigger chance to score points if you keep throwing your darts.

Ultimately, precision provides an opportunity for repeatability: not even the best dart players can consistently hit the bulls eye, so if you are looking for solid revenue streams and regular deals flow, I believe this is where you have the better chances to get them.

FIVE WAYS TO ENCOURAGE STRAY SALES

"Insanity is doing the same thing over and over again, expecting different results." –
A. Einstein

Sounds familiar? This is how most sales organizations work. As a new fiscal year approaches, the sales planning sessions start. Although we know that past performance is no guarantee for future success, still we project the previous year's sales figures into a dry formula to determine a growth rate for our business, based on more or less proxy market and client opportunities, and come up with figures that will hopefully please our managers.

Then we build sales plans that are lifted verbatim from the past. Just like the quote from our modern physics genius, we do the same things over and over, expecting different results. The point is: we should not. We should look at how ants work.

Ants have a built in mechanism to find the shorter route to food. They communicate with each other leaving trails of pheromones that can be followed to reach it, and then lead the ants back to the colony. Once the route is established, every ant will reinforce it by depositing more pheromones.

Your sales teams should apply the same technique to make sure that your portfolio of products and services is exposed to your best source of food – the client – by driving the sales colony there. It doesn't matter if the path is a beaten one – a client that you have visited many times already – or a fresh one. The key is that the route to your food is marked, enforced and exploited by the community. Think client penetration rates and share-of-wallet.

An even more interesting ants behaviour has been observed by some researchers. A few adventurous insects will break with the rules right away, and intentionally avoid following the pheromones scent. Instead they choose to take an alternate – longer and often more dangerous – route to the same stash of food. These ants do that to establish an alternate path to be used in the event of the first one becoming unavailable. This way, adequate food supply to the ant colony is always ensured.

I find this conduct clever, very clever: break from the norm to ensure sustainability of a resource scarce by definition. Think of your sales teams searching for different routes-to-market or innovative sales channels to reach your clients. How many times do you, as a sales manager, foster the breaking of the rules at the very beginning of your fiscal year? I bet you only do it – if ever – when your numbers are not adding up and it's probably way too late to make any impact. More probably, you just rely on the good old way of doing things, the one that always served you well in the past. Well, in case you haven't noticed the world has changed.

Finally, ants are also unique as they may be the only group apart from mammals where interactive teaching has been observed and documented. Some species go on food quests using a process called "tandem running". A pair is established, consisting of a leader and a follower, where the follower obtains knowledge through its leading tutor. Both leader and follower are acutely sensitive to the progress of their partner, with the leader slowing down when the follower lags, and speeding up when the follower gets too close.

In sales terms, this is of course the none-too-often used methodology of tutoring young sales reps by pairing them with your more senior and expert professionals. Truth is, with the current sales churns, urgency on generating short-term revenues and manic focus on quarterly – if not monthly – results, young sales reps never have a chance to be properly guided through the best route to your best clients. You're fine until your senior sales executives jump ship.

By applying some of the techniques above, I truly believe that you as a sales manager could drive significant innovation, improvement and better results too. If nothing else, just ask yourself: "How do I make sure that an alternate supply of revenues is made available just in case the main one gets dried up too soon?" Then, encourage your sales team to be creative:

1. **Choose your best route.** Identify early on, ideally at planning stage, an alternate path to test new products or services, to sell indirectly something that your company

has traditionally always sold direct only (or the other way around) or to introduce and launch any new product. If you discover a cheaper way to deliver great value to your clients, don't be tempted to keep everything for yourself as better margin. Pass most of the savings on, grow your top and bottom line.

2. **Drop your pheromones**. Exploit word of mouth. Even in the enterprise space people talk and are influenced by others' feedbacks and recommendations. CEOs and CIOs do talk to their peers often and quite candidly too. Start a client centred social media program to cater for your key customers and users, and use it to delight them. Deploy your best sales resources, and don't forget to let everybody else know.

3. **Get marketing to write more and better stories**. Success stories are overrated, make them un-success stories. Failure stories, scaring people into action. It actually works! Clients can learn a lot more from their peer's (or their industry's) failures than successes. Make those stories easy to re-tell.

4. **Let failures drive more action**. Failure in others stimulates our own pride: "I'm sure I could have pulled that off, and I'm gonna show the world how!" Success of others can cause envy and self doubt: "My company is too big/too small to replicate that success", "Our market is too small/too big", "Our product is too complex/too simple", "I'm not good enough", "My team is not good enough", "Our leadership will never approve of this". The list of excuses

is endless. Use the leverage of failures to make more things happen. The more radical, the better.

5. **Reward the how**. When managing your sales teams' performance, do not only reward the absolute sale value but reward also how the sale was completed. Good sales open doors for more business, bad sales shut them down and leave behind corpses and bad feelings.

Eventually, by encouraging what I call *"stray sales"* you will be able to overcome the rigidity of an outdated sales planning model and of an aged sales behaviour, and start driving your sales teams toward creative and innovative ways to success.

Mimicking the behaviour of ants and applying it to technology is of course not a new notion. In fact, leading technology companies are using it to develop products like network routing algorithms and cyber security software.

But I think that the application to sales and sales teams is even more interesting, intriguing and relevant.

YOU CAN LEAD A HORSE TO WATER...

... but you can't make it drink. What happens when your sales teams are not thirsty?

Sure, sales compensation is usually largely tied to actual sales. However the definition of "a sale" has changed through the years. Not so long ago, sales was measured on orders. This was the good old times (if you were in sales, that is) when you could just wait until the very last hours of the last day of the quarter to bring in the magical signed order, cash your commission and start planning your next vacation to the Maldives or Acapulco. Only at a later stage would management painfully discover that, in many cases, it could take months for the company to be in a position to actual invoice those orders, and longer still to book the associated revenues. So the obvious solution was to measure sales on revenues.

I guess we are all familiar with the sort of discussions that this new metric brought in. Sales complaining of inability to book revenues because of products failing to ship, undelivered services or failure to meet service level agreements, and so on. All problems, by the way, many companies are still facing today. Then came the latest trend: measure sales on revenue and margin. Now, this opened up a huge discussion around cost of sales, cost of fulfilling (including, in the case of products, manufacturing and shipping) or, for services, delivery cost.

Still, we would expect that at least sales should still feel thirsty right? Well, actually you'd be surprised to discover how many sales reps, especially those assigned to enterprise class clients, do not always show the degree of proactivity that thirsty people should show.

So we often end up in a situation where it doesn't really matter if marketers or business developers bring fresh clean water to sales, they still won't drink. Just like a wanderer in the desert, they might not realize how thirsty they are. In extreme cases, they will not even feel any stimulus of thirst. But fact is, failure to drink will cause dehydration and make them sick, sometimes beyond recovery. And with them, your company too.

The point I'm trying to make is that sales teams should be thirstier than ever. The battle for customers and revenues is fierce out there, and no company can relax. Every prospect your team is not touching is a lost opportunity, every dollar that clients don't spend with you, they will spend with a competitor of yours.

I believe that one of the problems is that quite often, in the attempt to aggressively drive the sales teams, we end up pointing a fire hose at them, and most often than not run the risk of drowning them. Think of the amount of data – sometimes information – marketers regularly throw at sales reps. Portals, corporate blogs, audio, video, newsletters, training sessions. Endless and convoluted emails full of URLs & pointers to more data. Fifty slides powerpoint presentations, font size 9.

I specifically think that most companies have a huge knowledge management problem. Mostly unrecognized, at best thinly disguised behind the production of a huge corpus of collateral material generated in industrial sizes. Because we can build and deliver a ton of sales materials, we do. Rather than measuring what is really used – hence useful – we measure how much we produce. Expensive, inefficient and wrong.
Oh and by the way, the answer is no – notwithstanding what some might think - big data will not solve the sales-marketing problem and will definitely not make sales thirsty, quite the opposite actually. If anything, *we need better data.*

SELL WITH YOUR SOFT SKILLS

Sales reps need to keep developing and honing their sales skills, both product and – arguably more importantly – soft skills. Too many bad companies staff their sales training centres and universities with the wrong teachers.

Have you ever heard the expression: "Those who cannot do, teach"? It's an old and well known saying. I guess that today it should sound like "Those who can't sell, consult". The point is, too often we pay attention to people that tell us what to do without them having done it themselves. There's no way they know how to do it, or why. I suspect most of the consultants fall into this category.

Sure, they have blueprints and frameworks, 2 by 2 charts and enchanted (!) quadrants. But doesn't it sound like a get-rich-quick scheme? Something like "here are the instructions on how to make a million dollars, I guarantee you it works, I'm letting you know because I'm such an altruist person"? Give me a break!

What about sales skills? I think we all agree that a sales person needs a certain set of skills, right? Some knowledge of the products being sold – and this is usually pretty straightforward and easily taken care of. But also a set of "soft skills". You know, the "art of negotiating", "getting to yes" and the sorts?

Now, it seems to me that this sales toolset gets often overlooked or taken for granted. Worse, often we just send sales reps to sales universities full of teachers who never actually sold anything – let alone complex IT projects – to anybody, and expect them to pass on the wisdom. Why? Why can't we get great "real" sales people as teachers?

The answer is simple: because great sales people remain sales people all their lives. They don't want to pass on their skills. They want to keep selling. Products, services, ideas, dreams even. It's what drives and fulfil them. Is theirs a set of skills that can be taught? Of course. But stellar sales reps do not necessarily want to.

Or more often than not, they do not know how to. Hence usher in the "professional teachers". I think we need to break this deadlock.

MODERN MERCENARIES: THE SALES REPS

Sales reps are mercenaries (I know - I've been one). They are from many angles already, so let's stop pretending they work for the good of the company. Sales reps only understand one word: commissions. And they work for themselves.

I believe that it's much better to have a clear, strong and powerful lever - i.e. $$$ - than pretending to have many weak ones. It's a lot more honest too.

What do we usually tell our sales force? Stuff like:

- go sell the whole portfolio of products and services to our clients
- work in the interest of the client
- position the company strengths first
- focus on value for the client and the company

That's a lot of wishful thinking, if you ask me. What they will understand is: let's sell the stuff with the highest commission, that will generate recurring ones and that's easier/faster

41

to sell. And yes, expect them to often oversell what the company can provide, or try to sell what the company can't provide. And of course to discount it wildly.

Sales reps have very basic needs: show me the money and give me something to sell (in that order).

This is also reflected in the fact that whenever sales is forecasting below target, we tend to build quick extra-rewards or special prizes to steer their behaviour. So in essence, rather than changing the product (or pricing it more aggressively, or packaging it differently) which they just can't sell fast enough, we offer to pay them more if they try harder. This of course is a completely fine strategy if you have 100% confidence in your product portfolio, but who does?

The large majority is quite happy for you to just pay their expenses, let them drive powerful cars and turn a blind eye on the occasional "disappearing act" on Friday afternoons.

Sure you can put together all sorts of metrics, dashboards, sales life-cycle measurements, shape of funnels and pipeline reviews, deal velocity and win/loss ratio calculations. But are these measures really making them more successful? My guess is that they don't. What they do, however, is to make the sales managers feel better. It gives them the feeling of being in control, on top of things, whilst in reality all they do is to frustrate most sales reps in the conscious or unconscious attempt to micromanage them (a BIG no-no). Anyone sitting in regular weekly sales forecast meetings and reviews know this for a fact.

Instead, the most obvious lever you can use with sales is money. You don't sell what the company needs you to sell? First few quarters, you get very little money (how about 20% of your base salary?). You carry on like that, you're out.

But if you do sell your quota, or even better if you overachieve it (but not too much, I never trust figures like 150%+ of quota, it simply means that the quota assignment was wrong or that a one-in-a-lifetime lucky strike happened. Hence, quota overachievement should be rewarded with a different mechanism) then you get real bucks.

A word of warning though: if your orders don't turn into revenues as expected, then I'm going to reclaim your money back. Additionally, this will also avoid the typical case where sales reps try to sell something the company doesn't have in its catalogue, because they know that to be successful short term (thus to make money and keep working for this company) they need to sell what the company has right now.

In summary, I think you need to leave breathing space to sales reps to do what they can do best, i.e. being top hired guns or mercenaries, and to deliver against what they really want. Yes, that's money. Everything else around it – customer satisfaction, long term relationship, etc. – should be managed by different professionals, not necessarily on sales quota.

Evangelists for example, that in Guy Kawasaki's own words are "the purest form of sales". Let them be what they want to be and do not burden sales reps with admin tasks. Empower them to deliver stellar performances and reward them accordingly, but don't ask Sales reps to be something they never wanted to be in the first place.

Historically, mercenaries and soldiers of fortune have helped build countries and govern empires (some still do, like in the Vatican). Just accept that and make sure you get the best you can.

SALES: NOT AN ART, NOT A SCIENCE

I believe that sales, any kind of sales, is neither an art nor a science. It only took me fifteen years to come to terms with it. Now, if I wanted to give myself a lot of self-importance, I would compare this process to the most famous geniuses that across their entire lives went through a similar experience.

Or I would point you to the great book by Steven Johnson "Where Good Ideas Come From: The Natural History of Innovation", where one of the main topics covered and analysed is precisely the need to incubate your great ideas for a fairly long time before sharing and publishing them in full (think of Newton, Darwin, and many others).

But being a fundamentally modest guy, I will just try to articulate what I mean by saying that sales is neither an art nor a science. I have worked in and around sales across industries for almost 30 years, and believe me – I have seen a lot of action and heard a lot of explanations and theories about what sales is.

One party would have you believe that sales is an art.

The great salesman is the one that works on his own, applying his genius and magic touch to the way he relates to customers and executives. He was born with a special set of capabilities that he doesn't have to hone. As long as you pay his expenses and princely bonuses, he guarantees to deliver. However, don't ask him to participate in training sessions, study the new material on your share-point or even write a detailed sales account plan. His magic needs to be free from all these constrains, and discipline is a term he claims not to know the meaning of.

The opposite party would try to convince you that sales is a science. Describe every step of the sales cycle in the most minute details, develop and use dashboards to map tens of variables and elements that can influence a sell, report on a weekly basis and scorecard everything. Detail products from every single angle, feature, whys and why-nots, depict an accurate competitive positioning, identify each silver-gold-plutonium bullet to beat the competitors, dwell into financial tools and cost of ownership. Train like crazy and split the hair at every sales step. If you ever miss your numbers, you can always explain why, in 3D and using plenty of spreadsheets, graphs, mathematical models and Nostradamus predictions from 500 years ago.

Since the sales artist never makes it into management, you always end-up with sales scientists as sales managers. Unless you are lucky and somebody not from sales gets appointed to sales management. But that almost never happens.

So you end-up with a sales-scientist turned manager that runs the team. She would like to have more artists in her team, because she knows they are reliable and they will - somehow, please don't ask! - deliver. But she also knows that it's much easier to manage sales-scientists, at least she will have plenty of professional looking reports to submit to the VP for her next review.

Now, my point: I believe that sales is neither of the above. I believe that sales is a craft.

As an example, look at plumbers, shoemakers, builders, or any worker engaged in a given craft, and you will notice something very important they all have in common: a solid grasp of the base-rules, the basic mathematical formulas and physics notions they need to master their craft. But they also possess the capacity to improvise a lot, something the best ones keep doing day after day after day.

They apply real-life experience, they experiment and fail a lot, they constantly make decisions based on proxy data or no data at all (aka gut feeling), they quickly find impromptu solutions and fixes, even building tools that don't yet exist if needs be. They possess a special mix of theory and practice, they know the rules but deliberately choose to ignore them at times, they have inside knowledge but foster lateral thinking. They are driven by passion for delivering the best possible end product. They have a sound understanding of cause and effect, and can tell you how their business is doing without having to resort to dashboards and weighted averages, and build on that.

So next time you are in a sales meeting, work on your quarterly sales plan or spend time pitching a potential client, think of how you approach your sales activity. Are you really an artist? Do you feel like a scientist? My suggestion is that you should become the best possible craftswoman. If you are a woman, that is.

3. FINDING (AND KEEPING) CLIENTS

Finding clients is tough. Arguably, keeping them is less tough (note that I'm not saying "easier"). Losing them, is really simple. Unless you have a clear way to segment and address your client needs in a way that is relevant to them - and not necessarily aligned to your product portfolio or geographic coverage or whatever other internal indicator - you are in trouble.

How can you expect to sell a one-fit-all product in today's marketplace? Do you really believe clients and prospects will apply the same lens and perspective you use when looking at your company from the outside-in?

Social media tools and techniques have changed the way companies reach out and engage with clients forever, still many large corporations either do not use them or timidly start exploring only now how they could benefit client proximity and understanding. There are potentially many reasons for it - e.g. Corporate culture resistance to change, fear of the new, broad business risk aversion - but I believe that the upside of using social tools way outweighs the potential disruption to the company organisation or even internal power plays.

However, one must remember that tools are just that: tools. I can buy all the tools needed to carry out open-heart surgery (well, most of them!) and learn how to use them, but this will not turn me into a qualified surgeon to perform the operation.

That's why even before using social media, one needs to make sure that the overall approach to clients and markets is really being changed. That requires training, focus on the right activities and a lot of business common sense.

PRESENTATIONS INTO STORIES

How many times have you been at a work event or presentation and felt the impulse to stand up and tell the presenter "please stop wasting my time"? I bet that – if you are anything like me – too many times to count.

I'm going to tell you a secret: I love storytelling. I believe storytelling is the best way to learn, engage and relate with people. It's also highly entertaining, which doesn't hurt when you have to spend many hours listening to somebody talk.

That's why I see no reason why corporations should not be great storytellers too. Too often, however, in a corporate setting, things go wrong very quickly.

Think of the following:

1. **Have you ever tried?** Close your eyes and go back to the last time you heard one of your top corporate executives speak. Can you remember any of the three key things she said?

2. **Details kill attention**. Look at this chart:

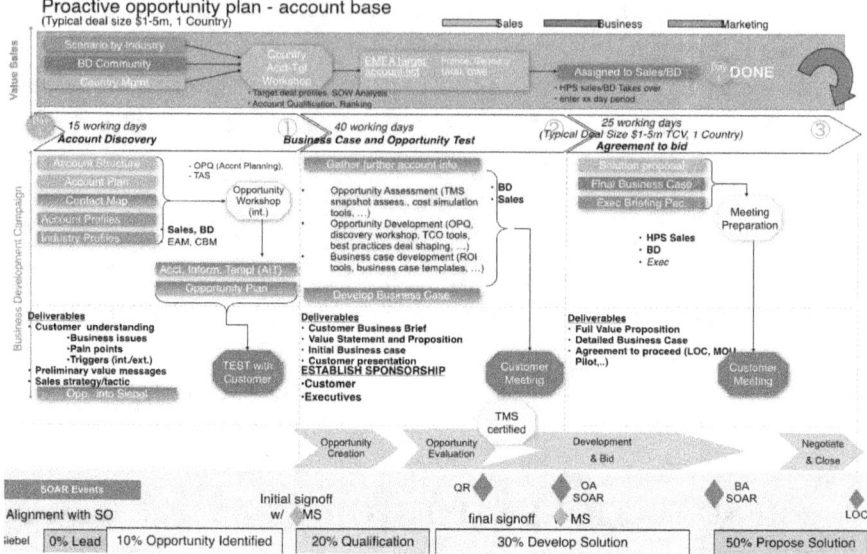

What do you expect me to remember after you're finished presenting?

3. **Ten priorities = no priority**. Most executives I know kid themselves. A list of 10 priorities is just a laundry list. nobody can achieve anything meaningful with more than TWO clear priorities in mind. Better still if you have only ONE. If you tell me your one priority I will remember it and contribute.

4. **You have all my attention, for the whole 60 seconds**. I suffer from a very short attention span. I know a lot of people do too. This means that we pay 100% attention to something, but not for long. So you'd better have good material to share or a very entertaining way of presenting it, else we will just switch our brain to something else.

5. **It's always the presenter's fault.** I think Guy Kawasaki articulated this best in his "Reality Check" book. In essence, anything that can go wrong during a presentation is utterly and completely the presenter's fault.
   - If the projector doesn't work, it's your fault.
   - If your pc does not synch up with the projector, it's your fault.
   - If the PA system/microphone doesn't work, it's your fault.
   - If your slides are hard to read, it's your fault.
   - If the audience tweets their way out of sheer boredom, it's your fault.

Why can't we tell stories anymore? And why is it so difficult for corporations and in business situations?

My grandma was a great storyteller. She would sit down with me on the porch in the long summer evenings and tell me stories about her youth. In the early '20s and soon after getting married, she left jobless post-World War I northern Italy and crossed the border into Monte Carlo, looking for work and a better life. My dad would grow up there and only return to Italy when he was thirteen years old. Grandma had so many amazing stories to tell, about living in a foreign country, meeting new people, learning a new language and way of living, missing her relatives back in Italy and about the shock of coming back to a post-war torn country where everything had to be rebuilt from scratch.

But the fact that she lived an amazing life was not the reason why she was capable of telling stories so vividly, and in such a way that would bring to life places and people and make you hang on every word. I think she had a distinct ability that older generations had, one developed out of necessity. A life that did not figure television, little or no radio, but many endless long nights in front of the fire sewing or doing other chores. A perfect setting for telling stories to make the hours go faster.

If you think of your own youth, I bet you were at some stage an equally awesome storyteller. You would invent games with the other kids, dream up the wildest adventures and fantasize with your friends. All those are key components of a great storyteller of course, and the good news is that we still have those deep inside of us. The bad news is that society and social rules have effectively discouraged and stigmatised our willingness to build and share those stories, especially in a professional or business setting.

But there's hope. Even large, conservative mega enterprises are starting to realise that companies unable to tell stories are just going to miss out on the rich and exciting social media phenomena, and the immense benefits that it can bring to their business development, growth and ultimate health.

If you believe in the power of storytelling, this is the time to go talk to your boss and demand to be blogging, tweeting and writing on people's Facebook walls on behalf of your company. Don't be shy. Everybody loves stories. And the only way you have to prove it is to tell them. I believe this is one of the very last cases where "if you build it, they will come". And your stories will be told, re-told and will become other people stories, grow and become new stories altogether. That's how magic happens.

A MARKETER'S OBSESSION

Are "fast" and "right now" better than "thorough" and "as soon as we have all the facts"?

Marketers are very familiar with the saying "what doesn't get measured, doesn't get done". Likewise, we are fairly accustomed to spending a great amount of time on data gathering and analysis before making any decision. On one side there is the need to collect "facts" or "data": this activity alone caters to our rational inner-self, the side of our brain that wants to be "informed" before making a call. We want to know how big the market is, how many potential customers are sitting in a specific industry sector, how much they spend on our products or services.

Often this process can take a long, long time and just as often we end up with such a huge amount of data that we struggle to turn into information, and that - in turn - into intelligence.

But that's ok, after six months of analysis we launch pretty much the same thing we would have launched in only 1 month, but we revel in the comfort of having done our (expected) homework. So when the marketing campaign will fail to produce the expected results, we will have our data-gathering activity to justify our failure. Because of course, as a side dish to the six months analysis, we will have developed a beautiful 25 dimension by 7 elements rolling weighted dashboard that will keep us on top of everything.

Only, we will spend most of our energy there rather than pushing the marketing campaign we developed in the first place!

In the opposite camp, we know that in the current business context, fast is almost always a winner. There are plenty of examples of companies shipping 80% or so finished products, and then iterating to complete and fix them at a later stage. I think you need a very strong attitude to do that, what with all the bean-counters and spreadsheet-based managers that you have to overcome to just ship!

But I also think that at end you might actually get better results from your gut-feeling based initiative rather than from a full-fledged, research-based, several months long preparation. If nothing else, you can churn much faster and try many different things in the time it took you to go the "safe" way just once.

And about measurement: who cares if you cannot build patterns and paint cause-effect behavioural models, as long as you ship and customers buy what you do? Give your marketing campaign everything you've got first, then figure out a way to measure what happened and turn it into a learning experience.

Especially in large corporations, we are losing the ability to pay attention to our instincts, experience, inner-voice or gut feelings, whatever name you want to call it.

Not only that, most experienced and battle scarred executives and professionals actually fail to embrace a new way of doing things, effectively putting up barriers to innovation and change. The young breed soon develops the same risk averse mentality and before we know it,

they're ruined forever. I believe that as leaders
we need to change this.

We need to foster and nurture new ways of
accepting, embracing and even seeking risk. Great
ideas are never fully baked at inception, so no
matter how accurately you choose the ingredients,
you won't know the result until you get your dish
out of the oven and in front of your customers.
That's what counts.

DELIVERY RULES

Marcus Tullius Cicero, Roman philosopher,
statesman, lawyer, political theorist,
constitutionalist and one of Rome's greatest
orators stated that *"delivery of a speech is much
more important than content"*. So why are we
building over-detailed presentations and business
plans, endeavouring to back them up with endless
amounts of data and "facts"?

Steve Jobs was probably one of the greatest
business speakers of all times, a master of
"pause to effect". Whilst certainly equipped with
exceptional natural skills, Jobs actually spent a
lot of time alone practicing and practicing and
practicing his speeches until they were perfect.
Then he would come on stage and do his thing
effortlessly.

I think Guy Kawasaki is another great
speaker. He's a master in streamlining contents
and making sure you don't get killed by
information overload at the second slide. His 10
(slides) – 20 (minutes) – 30 (point font) rule is
apparently simple, but actually requires a lot of
work to be obeyed.

Delivery is everything. Content is certainly
important, but it's second to context itself. In

the words of Alan Webber (author of "*RULES OF THUMB*") context is how we make sense of the world.

But if your delivery style is plain or even slightly boring, what will happen is that any good content will go unnoticed and the context will make no sense as people will already be thinking about something else three minutes into your speech.

So make sure you work on your delivery techniques first and foremost, strengthen your presentation or speech context setting and only then work on the contents. We in the audience will be grateful for that.

PUSH TO OPEN

To enter a house, shop or office almost anywhere in Europe you need to push the door in. Curiously, in the USA (and I'm sure in many other countries) you almost always have to pull the door out to enter. I'm told that apparently this amounts to a key security feature, in order to allow a fast exit from a building in an emergency (fire, earthquakes, etc.). This simple observation made me think about businesses and how they try to entice and attract customers' attention.

Retail is a good example of pull techniques: dear customer please come into my showroom, let me offer you a free download from my website, do sit in this comfortable leather chair and use our free wi-fi while you wait for your car to be serviced.

Online ads, e-mail and snail campaigns are a (sometimes not so) good example of push: dear customer, I just don't care what you are doing right now so I'm going to interrupt you anyway, too bad if my message is not relevant to you. So "pull" seems to be more a customer choice to come and see, "push" is more interruption and company centric. Or is it?

The intriguing thing for me is that it doesn't necessarily have to be that way. Shrewd marketers know that if you manage a good combination of the two you can really build a stronger customer experience and get their attention in a way that actually makes sense to them – not to you only.

Permission-based online campaigns do work, especially if you really listen to what your prospects are interested in and don't overextend the permission to interrupt that you were originally granted. Likewise, your shiny packages and cool shop layout might actually pull a lot of people through the door, but you'd better have a way of very quickly understanding what will make them stay in the shop and actually go beyond browsing the shelves.

I think the key is to mix and pace your push and pull techniques across your marketing campaign, and give a chance to prospects to choose which one works best for them.

Customers have so much choice today that they can really just ignore you, but at the same time they often need the right "stimulus" to get into motion, push and pull marketing can do just that.

ARE YOU CATERING FOR FARMERS OR HUNTERS?

A while ago Seth Godin posted an interesting piece called "Hunters and Farmers", that inspired me to write this paragraph, with the objective to elaborate a little bit on the concept.

Particularly intriguing is his point of view that if you are in marketing, you need to have a clear understanding on who you are marketing to.

The two groups use – and need – very different tools. And what you use to hunt – say bow and arrow – is really useless for a farmer, although arguably you can use a spade to fight your way through.

Hunters are usually seasonal, just like customers ("the game") can have very different needs depending on their "season".

For example, they might be looking to save money, planning to expand operations, or to deploy a new growth initiative.

Expanding on this view, there's the additional aggravation of potentially hunting for new business on pristine (for your company) ground that might turn out to be the farming ground of another company. You may need in this case an altogether different approach.

Farmers may want to sow the seeds looking for additional business on their farm (aka installed base of clients) for a portion of the year, and at a later stage go hunting looking for new-new business on unexplored customer segments and geographies, or whenever installed base business is soft.

As an example, if you are marketing IT support services, you typically have a window of the last couple of months of the year plus the next two months of the new year to farm your customers, looking usually for contract renewals, but then you have to switch into hunting mode and look elsewhere for further business growth.

Farmers may also want to look at crop rotation, i.e. cross-selling services and products to installed base customers according to the "seasonality" of their needs. A good example is customers demanding IT usage peaks for special projects or for busy parts of the year (e.g. Christmas online shopping).

Hunters should always be ruthless, to get themselves the best chance of success – after all, a fair and friendly hunter is unheard of. So marketers should be providing the ammunitions to make a big and quick impact, making them as effective as possible to catch their prey. However hunters should also be mindful of not destroying their hunting grounds, by killing or turning off potential clients because of an approach too bold or disruptive.

TYPICAL TRAITS OF HUNTERS:
- They experience long periods of "distracted noticing" interrupted by brief moments of "frenzied panic"
- Are easily distracted, because noticing small movements in the bush is exactly what you need in hunting
- Given a desk job, they freak out
- If promoted to internal sales they will fail
- Want to try stuff and see what happens
- Want high-stakes missions
- Fit better into long sales cycles

TYPICAL TRAITS OF FARMERS:
- They are used to sweating the details, to be worrying about the weather and to choose seeds and breeding

- They are good at taking care of endless homework problems, just don't ask them to change gears quickly
- Don't dislike technology, they dislike failure
- Prefer productive meetings
- Are typically more popular than hunters with the economy
- Rely on other farmers

As in most things in life, striking the right balance of hunters and farmers in your sales team will be the key to your success.

Interestingly, clients themselves can be natural hunters or farmers. Marketers often confuse the two groups. Are you selling a product that helps farmers and hoping that hunters will buy it?

Finally, a reflection on entrepreneurship. One of the paradoxes of venture capital is that it takes a hunter to get the investment and a farmer to patiently make the business work.

YOUR CUSTOMERS ARE OUT THERE, SOMEWHERE

Even the most senior and experienced marketers will confirm it: identifying the right target customers for a company is still one of the most challenging endeavours you can think of.

For IT companies that are focusing their efforts on enterprise-class customers, it can quickly turn into a nightmare. My ten years tenure in the marketing department of a leading IT company has left many scars, among the biggest ones is the sense of frustration at the inability to really identify - in a quick and accurate way - who are the potential customers out there.

In my experience, the concurrent causes to such an outcome are fundamentally two: failure to properly implement and use CRM systems, and the lack of traction between marketing and sales departments.

CRM systems are great on paper, but unless you have a rigorous data consistency check policy and procedures, soon run into a worthless ocean of data points which no analytics program can actual use to model or extract intelligence from.

The feud between sales and marketing is so old in the business world that it's almost pointless to try and identify who should lead or trail, or how one should feed into the other etc. Suffice to say that more often than not the two departments actually report into separate business units, with separate metrics and measurements (sometimes they even speak different languages it seems...).

So going back to the original intent of finding the right clients, what if we could apply some of those micro-targeting techniques to IT marketing demand generation campaigns?

After all, data quality and freshness is a problem all marketers have to face – and solve. Likewise, even if you are targeting large commercial companies, you still look for that special personal connection so that you can link into the highly relevant and emotional side of the prospecting buyer of your product or service. And then drive your sales team in a more precise – surgical? – way. Faster sales cycle. Lower cost of sales.

Two intriguing concepts to share:

1. **Adopt micro-targeting techniques for customer advocacy**: increase relevancy by using better

tools to improve customer data completeness and accuracy. Big improvement from collecting business cards at events, from pestering users of your website with endless forms before downloading any valuable information and from having score of telemarketers spending zillions of dollars to call uncooperative customers.As an added bonus, this could greatly improve your company's lobbying power: turn your best customers into your best advocates.

2. **Use micro-targeting to model your customer base.** I think there is an opportunity to use it as an iterative process, and build layers of information adding more details and perhaps nuances to each customer entry in whatever CRM system you use. Then you can start modelling what the target base would look like and ground your marketing campaign decision on more solid, accurate, fresh and reliable data points. Then go, get sales excited and execute on the campaign.

OUTDATED MODEL: THE FUNNEL
Once you have identified your clients, and reached out to them in a relevant (content and context wise) way, you're going to end up with a funnel of leads.

Now, I believe that this funnel is a very outdated model. It probably worked in the old economy, when sales steps were well identified sequential actions - e.g. build awareness, generate interest, create a lead, develop lead into opportunity, etc. - and attached activities.

The model breaks down in a hyper-connected, digitally engaged world, where customers are surrounded by information and have countless ways of learning about your products and services. Consumers can nowadays pull the information they want from anywhere, and not necessarily wait for marketers to push messaging to them. Additionally, clients who have considered your brand but failed to purchase in your funnel, could still become your advocate or, why not, future customers.

So it's safe to say that customers are not in a funnel anymore but rather on a journey. A journey that requires marketers to accompany them throughout the different stages with helpful, relevant and clear information, to help them evaluate and choose your company instead of your competitor.

These clients, if well catered for, will turn into influencers and even evangelists of your brand toward their networks of family, friends and colleagues.

WEED YOUR CLIENT BASE

As we have seen in the previous chapter, it's difficult to identify the right target customers for your business, especially when using incomplete or fragmented client and market information. Once you do establish a solid client base, you can start building the sort of long standing relationship that, if well managed, can provide years of valuable benefits to both parties.

One of the key elements to maintain a healthy client portfolio is to make sure that every now and then you weed it. Not unlike what a good gardener would do, so that the grass, plants and trees can grow healthier and stronger. In return, a tidy garden will be easier to maintain, please your eyes and senses and provide plenty of enjoyment for you and your dear ones.

Let's admit it: we all have customers out there who are dragging our business down. They are tough to deal with and to please, they consume a lot of our best people cycles - solution architects, project managers, sales reps, even execs - and don't really promise growth or additional future business for our firm.

These are the clients who are first to criticise and demand extras that either: *a)* you cannot provide or *b)* you can only provide by diluting your overall margin. They are also the ones who tend to be quite vocal when something goes wrong, but never say a word when everything runs smoothly.

Truth is, customers are not created equals. Just like companies are not all the same. I completely buy into the concept of "the market of one", but it better be the right one for your business.

So you need to take care of your clients. If you can, move them to a low-maintenance approach, where you can make sure that they are reasonably happy and don't stir pointless discussions.

More often than not - however - the best way is just to severe them. Cut them loose. Be honest; politely tell them that you are not interested in working with them anymore, help them find alternatives and just bid them farewell.

By doing so, you will ensure that you spend your and your organisation's time looking for and taking care of the customers and prospects that really count.

The ones who you can delight with your products and services, the ones who will come back for more and partner long term with your company to achieve great things together.

Eventually, by regularly weeding clients you will also be in a much better position to: focus your company on the most desirable business to be won, make better use of the resources and capabilities currently available, make better informed investment decisions.

Oh, and your margins will get a lot stronger along the way too.

4. WHAT PROBLEMS DO YOU SOLVE?

Our models just carry the present into the future. Everybody knows that's wrong. (M. Crichton)

It doesn't really matter if you are selling services or products, subscriptions or pay-per-use, simple or complex, local or global. What really matters is that you understand what problem you are solving. In any case, make extra sure you are not ending up with a solution looking for a problem (unfortunately the business world is full of those), because that would kill your business from the very start.

A great way to avoid that pitfall is to make something that you would use, something that you believe other people would use, and that would make their life better. Remember the old adage of better-faster-cheaper but make sure that you do not take shortcuts that would turn your idea into a dead proposition.

There are many ways to identify which problems need to be solved. The easier way is to ask your personal network: friends, colleagues, users, readers, fans. Listen to what they tell you, but make sure you distinguish between what they want and what they need. We all want something that we don't really need. Usually something we want only provides temporary satisfaction, mostly at personal level. Something we need, however, will help us work better, enhance our lifestyle, make us more productive, comfortable and ultimately change the way we behave. Its benefits will thus rebound from us to the people surrounding us.

Another good technique to identify what problems you are solving is to ask yourself why. Ask it frequently. If you are clear about the why of what you do then you're in good shape, because it's the relevance of the why that will, in due time, drive the what and the how. And once again, the rest is up to you.

SELLING IT SERVICES? THINK PRODUCTS

To all my readers, friends and former colleagues in the IT outsourcing business, here's a great tip for you: to grow your business, you need to make it easier for your clients to purchase your services.

The best way to do it, of course, is by mimicking the consumer products approach.

Anybody working in the IT outsourcing industry would be able to tell you about the tendency to over-customize services in this space. This behaviour always ends up in producing tailor-made proposals, regardless of the monetary value of the opportunity or indeed its technical complexity.

A $10m deal is usually assigned the same set of resources – business developers, pre-sales specialists, solution architects, sales reps, account managers, pursuit engineers – of a $500k deal, making it un-economical and ultimately un-healthy. Certainly unsustainable for outsourcers.

Statistical evidence shows that if you exclude a small portion of enterprise class clients, the large majority of companies would actually benefit more from pre-packaged and highly standardised IT outsourcing services rather than custom ones. Let's look at some of the benefits for both clients and outsourcers:

Client *key benefits:*
- Better price points
- Convenience in comparing (aka "shop-around" enablement) and purchase
- Easier dismissal or contract cancellation should quality/performance fail to meet expectations
- Modular flexibility and scalability (i.e. start small and grow as trust and convenience builds up)

Outsourcer *key benefits:*
- Economy of scale:
  - Maximization of IT infrastructure usage
  - Increased leverage of engineering resources
  - Lower cost to provide the service
- Faster time to market, by virtue of improved client targeting
- Lower selling cost (e.g. through the adoption of self-service portals vs. deploying a large number of "hunter" sales reps and picking up the associated cost)

- Easier to convey point-of-view
  - Straightforward articulation of client benefits and short term impact for the specific technical area being discussed
- Better win rates

One needs to keep in mind that behind an IT outsourcing proposition there is always – first and foremost – a financial decision to be made by the client. Typically, a comprehensive outsourcing evaluation requires a thorough due diligence process that can often be:

1. complex and time consuming (for both parties, client and provider of services)
2. expensive, if considering the time invested by people required to perform it and their lower productivity because of the added workload
3. potentially defocusing – or significantly slowing down – company operations for the duration of the activity.

Standardised IT outsourcing services, on the other hand, will neither require due diligence nor any significant investment of time and resources to evaluate them. These services would be pre-defined in nature (scope, technical specifications, service features, price) and limited by design in terms of flexibility. It is precisely their intrinsic rigidity that will constitute their best chance to be relevant to client's needs and hence successful.

At this stage you may wonder: it sounds like a good idea, but how does one build a credible, extensive yet simple portfolio of standardised IT outsourcing services? How do you develop and sell them?

SERVICES TURNED PRODUCTS

In my experience, the re-invention of IT outsourcing services requires a fundamentally different approach: outsourcing service providers need to switch from thinking "services" to thinking "products". The trick here is that across the key stages of design, engineer and build, outsourcers should mimic what product developers do. Let's take a closer look at the core development stages of a product.

DESIGN

Design of the service has to take place from the outside-in. What are the market opportunities? Which clients are looking for which services? If we build it, what sort of potential revenues would we be getting? Is there a clearly identified competitive differentiator that would give us a head start on the market? Is there a "disruptive" factor that we can introduce to change the rules of the game?

Once this analysis has been performed, the design team can sit down and get to work. The tools at their disposal are not unlike the ones that a product manufacturer would use. Factory equipment translates into technical capabilities of the support people and the IT tools they will use to provide/deliver the service.

When the design is completed – and of course there will be a number of iterations to ensure no deviation happens – the work is handed to the engineering department.

ENGINEERING

This is the stage where the team will look at the design specs and start thinking of how the different pieces – people, tools, processes – will gel together in a build-able product.

Engineering will also iron-out potential dead ends, isolating specific instances where the designed feature would not be economically – or even technically – implementable. In some case, they will need to make a judgement on the cost v. benefits of including that feature, and compromise if need be.

Most likely, at this stage the engineering team will attempt to build a prototype product of sorts – although with services this will obviously be a little trickier than with products. Best case would be if they could roll out a few of the service instances either to a few internal clients (non-production departments, for example) or friendly clients (early adopters).

The next player in the product development lifecycle is the factory.

FACTORY

Also known as the "build" stage, it is usually called the delivery function in IT outsourcing. The factory team needs to take the design and engineering specs and build a first batch of semi-industrialized products. They need to look at the technical and technological build-ability as well as make sure of the economical soundness of the engineering solutions. In some cases, the tools required to build the product will need to be developed from scratch, or adapted from previous versions. In many cases, the people who will deliver the product (keep in mind that we are using a similitude here, this is really a people-centric delivered service) will need to be hired or re-skilled.

It's highly likely that the factory team will push back on some of the engineering recommendations, and this will naturally trigger a back and forth discussion to reach some sort of compromise. All along, the design team needs to make sure that these discussions will not impact the nature of the product/service, as the tweaks and changes may turn it into something substantially different – and potentially less market relevant – than originally planned (descoping a product is always a risky proposition!).

Once the product is built, someone needs to take care of the next step: sell it.

SALES

Finally, the sales team needs to take the product and sell it. In this area, the adoption of product-selling techniques would greatly help too. Approach prospects with a clear and convincing PoV (Point of View). Challenge what clients say they want and position the relevant product as what they really need. Turn a long, difficult and intangible outsourcing proposition into something solid, real and short-term, highlighting how it practically benefits the customer. Scale the applicability of a standard proposition through innovative sales channels, like indirect and self-service for example, and aim at developing repeatable volume sales. Just like you would do with products.

GETTING IT DONE

I believe that there is definitely a huge opportunity in the standardised IT outsourcing services space, even more so if you design those services to be delivered from a fully automated cloud facility. Utility services play perfectly in this space.

Shrewd outsourcers will be able to rapidly build and deploy cloud-sourcing outlets, implementing along the way innovative mechanisms like real-time metering, dynamic pricing and wholesale utility provisioning. This is after all what is already happening in the application space, with salesforce.com historically leading the way as the first to provide SaaS and PaaS (nowadays obviously a very crowded space).

In turn, clients will get better deals: faster provisioning, increased relevance to their needs, more value for money, technology edge over competitors.

Outsourcers will be able to maximize infrastructure usage, retire non-selling services, develop innovative and more relevant services for their target clients and deliver better quality. Ultimately, their business will profitably grow.

Of course it's not going to be easy. There are geographic, economical and market maturity considerations that need to be accurately evaluated. Europe, for all its economic uncertainties, might actually be the best place for disrupting the IT outsourcing market. Historically, IT outsourcers have considered their highly customized services the best way to get reasonable margins, lock clients in for years on end and to sell more of their technology. All of that is changing very fast.

The players who are able to understand and implement a product-centric and cloud-based standardised model are the ones that will be charting the future of the industry, and reap the rewards.

THE PROSPECT OF BUSINESS

Doesn't it drive you crazy when you invest weeks or months pursuing an opportunity only to come out with zero business at the end? How about improving the way you prospect your market?

Simple question: in your company, who is looking for the right clients to go after? Sales? Marketing? Both? Nobody?

Chances are, there is a degree of ambiguity in the quest for the right opportunities and about who owns this process. This is why I think it's time to bring into play a new character: the prospector.

CHARTING UNKNOWN TERRITORIES

Prospectors of course acquired major notoriety with the 1849 Gold Rush in California, the one that captured popular imagination, and that so many frontier films have depicted.

Back then prospecting wasn't very scientific. It was a long and tiring process of traveling on foot or horseback, digging and panning, often with little or no results at all.

Today there are more sophisticated tools (like metal detectors for example) that simplify the life of the prospector. Efforts can be concentrated upfront, and waste of time and resources can be minimized. Machinery of course is taking care of the heaviest tasks of the prospector's job.

But back then life was tough and dangerous. Historically, mining prospectors did not really get much in exchange for their efforts either. As soon as traces of valuable minerals were found, word of mouth would bring in overwhelming swarms of gold diggers who pretty much stole the show.

Many prospectors were low skilled workers who operated in complete isolation, and that would move from area to area on the vague gut feeling of being on the right track. Even when they did strike gold (ah!), they were often exploited by more educated businessmen who would buy off the rights to excavate for little money.

Nevertheless the role of the prospector was a key one. His work would become the beacon others used to move around the country and chase their dream of wealth and prosperity.

Thanks to the prospector and the attention he would bring to a certain area, entire cities sprung out of nowhere, and hundreds of jobs were created. Think of the merchants selling food, tools and clothes to the gold diggers, of the builders of roads and houses, or the lumberjacks providing the building materials. Hundreds of thriving - even if short-lived -_communities were born. In short, the prospector was the instigator of wealth creation.

It's also worth noting that prospectors hardly ever turned into gold seekers, for example by setting up the infrastructure and methodically sift through soil or rivers searching for precious metals. Rather, they would cash on their prospecting discovery and move on to another area, often only after having squandered their little hard earned money on women and booze. So you could say that prospecting was a self-contained professional endeavour, one that required stamina, hunger for adventure and possibly a degree of restlessness, or love for a nomadic way of life.

BACK TO THE FUTURE

Fast forward to today's business context. Sales team's approach to finding the right clients and business opportunities on the market has not evolved at the same speed and degree of sophistication as the technological improvements. Notwithstanding the wealth of data points about clients and markets, most enterprise companies are still unable to process those and turn them into actionable information.

Adoption of data mining and big data processing tools will help, but it's going to take years before any of these very complex – and expensive – techniques make it into mainstream client targeting. Even on-line ads are still under-delivering on the promise of 100% target accuracy!

I believe that we need to bring into play a new professional role. One that directs costly resources to the right territory. A discoverer of gold nuggets. An enabler of focused efforts. We need a business prospector.

Look at the typical behaviour of modern day sales people. How many times have you seen sales reps spending way too much time on markets, clients or opportunities that were not really that solid?

One of the reasons for this is that sales reps are usually concentrating too much on the desired outcome of their activity – i.e. to close the sale – for actually performing the sales qualification stage in an appropriate way. Often, there is simply so much "wishful thinking" that their view gets dramatically distorted. The end result is committing far too much time and resources to non-existing business opportunities.

But what if we brought into play a true business prospector? Someone who, without the pressure of selling or winning deals, would professionally scout the hills of the international markets looking for traces of gold, silver and other valuable minerals?

To prospect in the right way, you really need to take a hard, dispassionate look at the opportunity/client. Is there a budget set aside for buying your product? Is there a time stamp on that? What is the urgency to buy? What is the real compelling event that could trigger a faster sale? Why us?

Prospecting also takes time. You cannot time box prospecting, because the next gold mine may be just inches away from where you are digging right now. It's an inherently inefficient job, that's another reason why sales reps cannot afford to do it properly.

It is a fact of life that sales reps might have a vested interest in pursuing an opportunity even when there is no real opportunity to pursue. For example, spending time on a top account, meeting and presenting or organizing corporate visits, is often seen as an investment into the future, building up "relationship".

The bad news is that it isn't really doing that. Gone are the days when you would build customer intimacy by dining and wining the client. Nowadays, what pays off in terms of building trust is to be up to speed with the industry and client's business model and needs, tell the client the hard truth, to express a well-informed and professionally sound point of view and to not shy away from tough discussions and - sometimes - confrontations.

Now, if you have not done your prospecting accurately and thoroughly, then you will simply not be in a position to do any of that.

BUT THERE IS HOPE

That's why I believe we need to bring back the prospector. Sales and business prospector as a new profession. One that requires market knowledge, business savvy, profound knowledge of the product/service your company is selling, hands-on experience and personal standing.

If you think of it, potentially quite an interesting proposition for the many jobless professionals pushing fifty who, because of the weird turn of the world economy, are finding it difficult to re-enter the job market.

It could even be an entrepreneurial opportunity, with teams of free-lance prospectors roaming the markets seeking the next gold mine.

Armed with best quality data mining and analytics tools, simulation software and business case templates.

It sounds a lot like the real California gold rush. Come play the game and choose your role: would you rather be a gold digger - the dreamer going for the big bang - or the guy selling shovels and picks - the long term oriented hard working merchant?

THE POWER OF ASSOCIATION

Music and sound are big players in our lives and they provide the backdrop for our days and nights. Ranging from annoying ones - like car horns and traffic noise - to disturbing ones - like alarms and emergency vehicles - it seems that we cannot escape sounds.

Sound can clearly influence the way we work, think and reason. Open space offices are notoriously noisy places and really low-efficiency ones too. It has been calculated that the productivity output of open-space office workers can be 60% lower than working in a quieter place.

City night sounds can turn our rest-time into a nightmare too, and more and more sleeping problems have been documented as related to those.

Fortunately we also have plenty of soothing sounds available to us. Nature is a great help in this space.

Chirping birds in the early morning have a tranquillising effect, signalling to our inner selves that everything in our world is well. The sound of sea waves is also very effective in taking us to a state of greater tranquillity and relaxation.

Music though is the real BIG player. Music can make us sad, happy, angry, and act as a huge driver, both ways, of our emotions. I strongly recommend you to watch Julian Treasure's TED speech to get more scientific evidence of this.

What I really find intriguing is how sounds and music can be used to support, enhance and in many cases even transform commercial brands and the related consumer's experience. Although at least a few major brands are using these techniques quite profitably since a few years (think of Coke's ads, Nokia's ringtone and Intel's jingle), I believe there is still plenty of space to try new things and improve.

Car manufacturers are also rather advanced in this space, although ironically many of them have a tendency to overdo the "emotional" focus and to sell – in many cases – what basically accounts to hot air, or the promise of an experience that – beyond the catchy music and spectacular visuals – really is not going to be true.

But what about business-to-business? How can we emotionally attach music to business situations, and use it to improve the outcome to our advantage?

Personally, I have always had the tendency, since a very early age, to associate songs or music to happenings, situations, people and emotions. I still do, and I find this association really helpful in bringing back the true nature of what I felt back then. For me it works even better when applied to people, as it recalls the emotional involvement experienced at the time.

Now, is there any reason not to use the same techniques within business situations and with business people? Why does a meeting, presentation or sales pitch have to be "emotionally dry"? After all, it has been proved that, given the complete equivalence of an offer from the technical and economical standpoint, even big name CEOs or CIOs will decide based on their gut feelings, or emotions.

In my view, there is no reason why business-to-business shouldn't use music and sound to increase the emotional awareness of their offerings, or at least to provide more tangible and emotionally rich experiences.

<u>HOW NOT TO BE INVISIBLE</u>

Phone conferences and meetings are notoriously low efficiency, hard to run and emotion-suffocating events. So why is everybody running more and more of them?

Every single company, irrelevant of its size, nowadays employs telephone conferences to control cost, by cutting down on employees travelling to meetings. In many cases these virtual conferences are perfectly fine and can straight on replace, with almost no side effect, costly in person events.

If run correctly, for example by applying strict discipline in terms of punctuality and duration, they can also bring some efficiency into the meeting. In fact, the chair person can exercise much more control than in traditional meetings, up to the point of muting participants' phone lines until his keynote is over (try to forbid everybody in the meeting room to speak instead!).

Unfortunately, in my experience and most of the time, they just turn into nightmares. One of the reasons I found is that people do not know how to behave in phone conferences. Meet the typical participants stereotypes, I'm sure you are familiar with some:

- the babbler: she never stops speaking, gives no chance to others to say something or to interject. She's got that monotone rhythm in her voice and seems to never quite get to the point.

- the mumbler: usually you can hardly understand what he's saying, almost talking to himself and not necessarily stringing together sentences that make any sense or have any consequence for anybody.

- the out-of-spacer: typically calling from a dodgy phone line, presumably mobile, dropping off often and just as often redialling in, causing the well known "beep syndrome" to the speaker, who usually ends up losing his thread.

You see, I think that having to rely on your voice only, without the richness of physical gestures or face expressions (or even your stance or just the way you sit) is an enormous limitation to how one can communicate.

Granted, video conferencing is slightly better than phone conferencing, although still rather awkward because through the webcam a speaker cannot really command the same attention that can be mastered in an in-person situation.

Unfortunately, I know a lot of people for whom phone conferences is the only way to meet. They actually never meet their colleagues in person, it's almost like working with virtual entities, which their mind tries to project into a real being by piecing together sentences and remarks heard through the phone system.

This cannot be good. Humans are meant to be interacting with each other. We are social animals, we need physical proximity – if not contact – to build confidence, strength and emotional empathy. Very little of that can be had through the phone. Tone of voice and accent can only convey a diluted subset of such a rich texture called in-person engagement.

On the upside, the phone system can work as a safety net for emotional people, for those who don't actually like speaking in front of others. Phone meetings can actually bring them the desired detachment from the audience.

By design, phone conferences limit the richness of the interaction and granted, this can actually be seen as a plus when too much interaction could jeopardize the meeting's direction or desired outcome. But I would still run the risk of ending up with only a half successful meeting but a much closer community of like-minded people, working, interacting and growing together.

Think about it in your next phone conference. Do you really like to be invisible?

FRUSTRATION AT WORK

In a professional world, there are behaviours that one expects to show. You cannot really throw a tantrum when you are frustrated by a colleague or your boss. So how do you vent your frustration and anger? Because sooner or later you need to, or it will build up and burst at the least convenient time.

I think you would concur that today's most common professional disease among white collar workers is stress. We live busier lives than ever, and we constantly have to increase our competitive skills on the many responsibilities that our jobs encompass. Our families require and deserve our full attention too, and life in a changing and more complex multi- racial society is becoming more and more demanding.

So how do we cope? And more importantly, how do we vent our frustration before it's too late?

Let's look at a typical work situation. The end of the quarter is rapidly approaching and the numbers do not look too good. You and your colleagues have tried every technique in the book, but simply to no avail. Your boss is adamant on her plan and simply does not want to listen to your suggestions. Deep inside, you know what should be done. Years of experience have given you the chance to live a similar situation before, and a radically different approach should be used to try and shuffle things for good.

But there's a problem. The other team members might have the same opinion as you, and some of them even tell you so, though nobody is willing to go against the boss. So you sit in endless meetings, fuming with stress and frustration building up inside. You want to shout people into some sense. You want to grab your spineless peers and tell them to fight for what they believe is right. But you just can't.

Companies expect your behaviour to be fair, politically correct. The whole concept of being a team-worker somehow limits the cards you can play when frustration reaches the red zone. So how do you defuse it? Because you know you have to, or you'll just explode.

One typical – and very human – reaction, is to just disconnect. As you realize your inability to fight the others any longer, you just distance yourself from the whole thing. This is bad for everybody – your team, your boss, your company –

because detached people do not give their 100% for the good of the business.

A second option, is to try and convince yourself that the others are actually right. In a large company, if you just comply and do as you are told, i.e. if you suck up to your boss, nothing bad can really happen to you. So just swallow your pride, put on the shiniest smile you can, and go with the flow.

A third option, which I actually choose quite a lot, is to document everything in a detailed and comprehensive way. It might sound tedious, but I have often built whole plans of action based on my own perspective on things, as if I was the one in charge. This, I found, has provided me a couple of interesting benefits: first, the simple act of writing everything down allows me to organize my thinking in a more straightforward way. Second, I can therefore build a more tangible piece of deliverable that I can either look at when the storm has passed – or the boss has been removed or the team dismantled, whichever comes first – or keep for my own use to look at a later stage and gauge if I was wrong or not. The learning opportunity is in any case huge.

Needless to say, it's never a good idea to send your action plan to your boss or her boss. Unless you want to put your job on the line (this has happened to me too …).

At this point you might ask: "What about your results? You would still miss them, right?". Well, the truth is that yes you might not really impact any short term improvement or corrective action.

But at least you would be able to keep your head together and avoid getting yourself into trouble. And that's rather an accomplishment already!

REPETITA IUVANT

"Things that are repeated help" the Latins used to say. I'm sure you are familiar with the "mind the gap" recorded message that you hear in a large number of tube stations in London (and in an incredibly large number of other cities too!). It's obviously a warning to travellers, suggesting them to pay attention when getting on and off the carriages. Regulars must be so used to it to the extent of not really hearing it anymore, having developed a brain filter to the repeating message. Less regular ones will certainly be grateful for the constant reminder.

Interesting how this technique can be applied to advertising and branding in the business world. We are all familiar with buzzwords and tag-lines. Some are good, some are bad, all are developed on the basis that the more you repeat them, the more people will believe them and ultimately do business with you.

However, a real risk exists for a "mind the gap" type of message: the risk of becoming "invisible" because of its repetitive nature.

In the London tube case it might lead to some nasty accidents. In your case, potential clients might disconnect from your brand as a form of defence, they might listen to your competitors' instead or they might just turn against you (annoyed customers do that sometimes).

The question is: "How do you strike the balance between repeating your message in a consistent way and keeping your clients attentively listening?"

Not an easy one for sure. Branding experts like Martin Lindstrom have written books on how to get inside buyers' minds, by appealing to their inner desires and flipping subconscious triggers to make them want your products. Interesting, but not necessarily applicable to the enterprise space.

Here you might need to come up with a more subtle way of projecting your branding message into one of long-term value for the client, or into a statement that by declaring what your company stands for, and repeating it consistently across a well planned advertising effort, will make the "why do you do what you do" much more tangible and real.

Curiously, politicians are also very good at exploiting the "repetita iuvant" effect, to the extent of ending up believing their own lies. But that's a different story, one that unfortunately centres on manipulation rather than on trying to convey a convincing truth.

Naturally, there are many other occasions beyond branding and advertising where this principle of repeating can apply with powerful results. As any student would know, a fundamental technique for education is repeating the material until it is "learned".

Closer to the business world, a typical example would be at events and presentations, where speakers might want to drive home a specific concept or issue that would really represent, in their view, the core message of their pitch. If you cleverly weave it into your slides, you will build a common thread across your material and will make it stand out from the crowd.

Once again though, careful not to overuse this technique: in the 21st century, with the information overload, infinite internet bandwidth and the seriously limited attention span of user and attendees, telling the audience what you are going to present, present it and then recap what you presented simply does not work anymore.

Finally, social media tools offer the ideal stage for a massive, and potentially extremely powerful, use of repetition as a way of driving home your message. The trick is to make sure that at every repetition you add some more value, additional layers of contents and context, to enlarge and enhance the core of your communication. Failure to do so, just like for the London tube, will cause your followers and friends to just ignore you.

5. (DO) REAL WORK

Email is not real work. Sitting in endless meetings or showing up at your desk 9 to 5 isn't either.

Unless you can pinpoint which daily activities are really adding value - to your clients, your friends, your family, your business, yourself as an individual - then you are not doing real work.

IF IT'S NOT BROKEN, BREAK IT NOW

The only way to really re-ignite a business model is to break it when it still works, so that you can look under the hood and change it.

I know: do not change the players if the team keeps winning games. That's the commonly accepted wisdom. Unfortunately though, I think that in the current business world this just doesn't apply anymore. Because of the unstoppable technology-driven innovation cycle, pretty much every major market is constantly and rapidly evolving, to the point that nobody can rest on success anymore, big or small.

You have to confront tight "windows of opportunities", dictated by season, market conditions or pure and simple recurrent business cycles, requiring your company to apply perfect timing to be in the best position to win.

Unfortunately, there are many very successful businesses that are actually based on a few core offerings bringing in 80% of the revenues or more, and that can therefore find it very difficult to develop radically new ones.

The pivot is a well-known technique that they can apply to instigate a major break with the past, by looking at side developments of a company's core business. What I recommend, however, is even more radical: it's about breaking what is working whilst it's working.

There are risks in doing this: your business might actually suffer in the beginning, and you might face criticism and pressure from investors and in some cases even from clients. But the mid-term benefits will definitely make those risks negligible.

Look at startups: most of them have perfected the move, quickly shifting their business core and focus to specific areas, sometimes part of the original mandate, other times tangential to that or even completely new. Famously, NeXT was primarily a hardware company in the beginning, that pivoted and became famous for its software (which in due time of course became OS X). That's just a top of mind example, there are literally hundreds of startups you can Google and checkout to see how the pivot(s) worked for them.

True, more established companies might find it very difficult to implement a counter-intuitive approach like this, especially when business looks good and revenues roll comfortably in. However, I believe that the best moment for driving major change is exactly when things go well, and not when you have to change because of business troubles. Too early is almost always way better than too late.

So what's holding big companies back? Conservative management, lack of leadership or clear strategic and execution intent, limited understanding of the market and its dynamics, fear, and many other factors.

But more than anything else I would say that the main reason is that those companies have forgotten a key rule of any entrepreneurship: risk always pays off, and those who embrace it as a way of business conduct will at the end come out on top.

So if your business is not broken, break it now. You'll learn a thing or two.

WHY MOST PRESENTATIONS SUCK

A presentation in a meeting or at an event is the beginning, not the end, of a conversation. So why are you bombarding people with copious and irrelevant information in your slide deck? And why are you so boring?

I know a lot of people who are much better presenting something in a phone meeting than in person. I guess they probably feel safer behind the artificial but solid barrier of a phone connection, strong in the knowledge that whatever happens they will not have to withstand the heat of physical interaction with real people.

When stepping on stage and given the task to present, even to an often moderate number of people, the phone-presenters typically move around awkwardly, stumble upon their own words, hardly look at the audience or stare fearfully into space when asked a question they don't necessarily understand.

As I routinely work on preparing slides and materials to support presenters and speakers for corporate events, I decided to develop a brief analysis of the main reasons why most of them, and their presentations, typically suck.

1. **You don't start with why.** We might care about what you do and even how you do it, but not for very long if you don't tell us why you do it. The why is the sustainable motivation for us to believe in your proposition.

2. **You talk too much.** I'm sure you like the sound of your voice, but we might not. Talking too much is definitely a sign of being uncomfortable, kind of using all the conversation bandwidth yourself so others cannot interject and cause you trouble.

3. **"Yes", "No" and "Don't know but I will find out" are all perfectly good answers,** which you never use enough. If you know your subject and are clear about its why, then in 90% of the cases you do not have to elaborate on a direct question, because you will have built a reply to that during your presentation, or you can follow up with more details at a later stage.

4. **You focus too much on what's missing** (features not available, slipping availability dates, etc.) and not enough on what is there. I see this almost all the time. As you start telling me what you do, you have the masochistic tendency to start listing the features that are not in your current product version, or those that will only be available later, etc.

5. **There's too much text on your slides.** Anybody can read faster than you can speak (unless you use fonts smaller than 10...), so please don't fill your slides with text. Slides are meant to be a support to your story, not the verbatim account and repository of everything you will say.

6. **The pictures you use are pointless** (i.e. slide fillers). This is a trend that is developing in the corporate space like a fungus. It manifests as high quality if pointless pictures of people and places that have, more often than not, no relation whatsoever with the topic being covered. Lately it's either a lot of highways and speed of light vehicles or incredibly complex and tall industrial and office buildings. I truly believe images can be much stronger than text. But you need the right image to express what you want to say or underline. Use similitudes, metaphors, epic, social and historical images to do that. And please stop showing pictures of sport teams!

7. **You don't have a story**. No matter how many slides you use, whether you start with why or not, whether your pictures are relevant or pointless – if you do not have a story, it shows. Worse, since nobody can remember figures and facts alone, your lack of a story or at least of a familiar context setting will make us completely unable to recall anything of your presentation.

8. **You cannot tell a story**. Let's assume you have built a reasonable story and that your slides are actually not too crowded, not too numerous and to the point. I can bet that most of the presenters would still lack the tone of voice, the gestures, the drive to engage and the ability to make that story resonate with the audience.

Great presenters are great storytellers, who in turn become great entertainers. Your business presentation should first and foremost entertain the audience, then captivate it and only then inform. Or it should at least disrupt the audience to the degree of them wanting to chase you out of the room!

So here's a couple of quick reality checks you can perform easily:

1. At your next event/meeting, ask any of the presenters if he's ready to go. Then just a few seconds before he gets on stage, switch all power to the electric outlets off. See how he performs with no slides and not laptop. You'll be surprised by the degree of paralysis the majority of speakers will fall into.

2. Next time you attend an event, listen to any one of the presentations. Then just after it's finished, without looking at the materials or your notes, try to re-tell the story covering what you perceived where the key aspects. Let a couple of days go by, then try again. Now take your reports and compare with the presentation slides. See how much you correctly recalled. If you run this exercise on a fair number of attendees, you will be surprised how many don't actually recall much. That's a sign of a bad presentation and/or a bad presenter. Or simply of the lack of a good story.

THE IMPORTANCE OF VELOCITY

Is your company going nowhere fast? You are not alone.

You see, I think that in business moving with speed is not necessarily always a good thing. What you actually need is velocity. Unfortunately, a lot of enterprises consistently mistake speed for velocity, in the illusion that if you are fast enough you will take advantage of early adopters and new market trends. Truth is, you need to know where you are going before you accelerate to reach it. Quite relevant to your business drive, I would say.

In essence and in general terms, velocity is a much more meaningful indicator than speed. Let's have a quick look at the definitions (source: WIKIPEDIA).

"In physics, velocity is defined as speed in a given direction. Speed describes only how fast an object is moving, whereas velocity gives both the speed and direction of the object's motion. Both magnitude and direction are therefore required to define velocity. "

So we have established that velocity means going somewhere at speed, possibly accelerating all the way but having first chosen a given direction where to go. This is key for a business. Choosing a direction means:

- Establishing your potential market
- Estimating which/how many clients to reach
- Defining the product or service your company will build and or sell
- Choosing a pricing policy: for example, cheap but broad reach vs. Expensive but narrow
- Deciding your geographical focus: I.e. global v. Local

Your business plan will have to articulate much more than this of course, but if you can start with clearing those questions marks then you are already on the way to a good solid start. Your aim should be to be in a position to carefully pick your fights and give yourself and your company a better chance of winning. A sound business plan should also enable your company to make the right investment decisions (tools, infrastructure, people, etc.) where it matters.

It should spell out your commitment (you should do what you say you will, when you said you would do it), and set the right expectations to your internal and external clients. Finally, your plan should identify an ecosystem of players and the associated responsibilities, accountability span, metrics and measures.

Failure to clearly document and articulate all of the above will enhance the risk for your business of going nowhere fast. Sometimes this can be acceptable, especially if you drive a company that is not afraid of failures for trying something really innovative, cutting edge and/or disrupting. If you embrace the risk of failing as a strategic element of what you do, then it's ok to fail fast and restart just as fast.

Remember though that there is a cost associated to this behaviour, and that it requires a lean and mean company to be able to learn from failures and quickly pivot to a different product, service or market approach (aka "a change of course").

FIRE YOUR BOSS

What to do when your managers are incompetent and do not listen to what you say? Put them out of their misery!

No, of course I don't mean killing them. What I mean is, after you have tried everything you can to help and make them understand, just ditch them. Fire them. Move to a different team, or quit if the management disease has spread too far.

I believe that for a company to have poor management and leadership is bad enough in normal times. With the current economic situation, however, it's plainly criminal. And I'm not talking about executive vice-presidents only. Actually, in my experience, it is where things are supposed to get done - i.e. at middle management level - that the lack of skills and attitude really makes the most damage.

So what are the typical signs of a poor manager?

BAD COMMUNICATION.
Meetings are badly prepared, no material is shared or circulated before-hand (often not even after the meeting), meeting notes are not taken and actions are neither captured nor tracked. Emails queries do not get replied to. Higher management communications and directions are not timely sent through the organization.

FUZZY ROLES AND RESPONSIBILITIES.
You can never know whether a specific task is really part of your duties or not. You know you should say "no" more often but you cannot figure out when.

NO DELEGATION.
Things get discussed without your knowledge or involvement, and decisions are made behind your back.
Growing frustration of team members.
Colleagues share their frustrations among them instead of taking them to the boss. By the way, this is what I call the "pioneer's dilemma", or "I would go first but I'm afraid of getting arrows through my back".

LOTS OF SURPRISES.
I've said it before, surprises in business are a very clear sign of bad management. Anticipating a

problem usually means you can fix it or at least limit the damage, being surprised by one – as in "no telling signs until the very last second" – always end up in disaster. When you get a lot of surprises, yes even positive ones, the writing is on the wall for your manager.

NEVER ENDING PROJECTS.
Problems are never solved. Processes are never fixed. You keep having to fix the same core issues all year long.
Planning activities last for months.
(Note: planning is a stage. Do it, spend the right amount of time on building your plan, then go and execute. Most poor managers seem to never be able to get out of the planning stage and into execution).

NO SKILLS AND CAREER DEVELOPMENT.
Team members do not get any support or assistance to develop new skills that would allow their career to develop.
So if you have the misfortune of having a boss showing any of the signs above, just do yourself – and him – a favour: fire him.

CORPORATE DISEASE #2
Setting the bar low enough so everybody can achieve the targets? Setting expectations so low that you will easily meet them? You are hurting your company, your team and yourself.
There is a disease that's spreading extremely fast across corporations. It's a deadly one, that turns teams and dedicated professionals into shells of empty apathy and useless people. It's called complacency.

It manifests itself through a yearly simple but tragic act: the bar setting. Usually incubated inside small minded old fashion middle managers, the disease develops in the format of setting goals ("the bar") so low that they will be easily achieved. Like a virus, once it finds a suitable host – aka the passive team member – it grows into 50 pages (or slides, or web pages, pick one) plans that:

1. Do not specify clear ownership
2. Do not make accountability clear
3. Set expectations at such a basic level that to achieve those becomes almost trivial.

Once the virus has attached to such people and plans, it's passed along to more people and makes its way into more plans, that also become infected with the same low-bar non-committal generic-sounding stuff. And then the disease goes in for the kill.

Nurtured by the middle management and nourished by the passive team of people, it disguises itself as just good enough to make the numbers and get the organization through another quarter. And gets into the minds, plans and speeches of the Vice Presidents.

At this stage it's way too late. So many people have been infected that there is no way to go back. Those of us that knew from the very beginning that the deadly disease was manifesting itself, have lost. Those of us who had the passion to change things on a much bigger scale, to challenge the status quo – including ours – have to conform or leave.

We who believe that to push people is to make them grow and develop into better people and professionals, have to admit defeat. Or write articles like this one to tell everybody to watch out for the virus. Don't give up. Fight for what you think is right. Put your passion into everything you do at work. Ignore the low-bar setters.

As per the one and only Michelangelo:

"The problem is not to set the bar too high and miss it. The problem is to set the bar too low and reach it too easily."

CHANGE THE WORLD

You are probably familiar with Eric Clapton's great song. Granted, it's a love song. The refrain goes "...if I could change the world...." and it made me think that actually we can all change the world.

And it doesn't necessarily have to be in terms of macro-stuff or mega-projects. There are small and nimble things we can all do every day to change the world one bit at a time.

Simple things like making people look at situations from a different angle, or propose a radically new approach to a business opportunity, or simply behave differently than in the past.

A friend of mine is trying to transform the big corporation she works for by selling added-value services through a low-cost sales force (as opposed to the dedicated direct-sale and specialist sales people). Another one is crowd-sourcing the translation of user manuals, tech spec and other customer oriented documents by reverse auctioning key projects.

A third one is setting up a coiffeur shop for ladies where she teaches them how to professionally bleach and arrange their hair, and then sells them the tools needed to do it.

I call them "professional agitators" and I'm convinced that we need more of them. People that are ready to scrap their old business "modus operandi" and re-invent a profession or job. Radical thinkers who are not afraid of introducing so much change into the system that they could actually lose their occupation.

I had a manager once, or should I say a leader, that I admired for his stamina, focus and continued innovation. He drove us so hard that at the beginning we all felt like we could not possibly bear the amount of change. But after a short while, we all embraced the approach and became a highly effective team of professional, achieving sterling results. When I asked him how did he know when the amount of change was enough, he said "when my own job will be made unnecessary, that's when".

I know what you are thinking, this is highly risky and not all organizations will like it. But you know what? If it's not risky, well maybe it's not worth our attention.

Complacency is the enemy a lot of us need to fight, and in the business world of today, the best way to do it is to stand up and try to change the world.

6. A MANAGER'S TOOLBOX

You need to have all your most important tools at hand. Just like surgeons. If you can't find the right tools, develop them. More often than not is just a matter of customising what's available so that it fits the purpose.

Once you have the right tools, use them consistently every day. Tune and tweak them little by little. Keep finding new ways to use them.

When the time is right, throw them away and get new, better ones. Start again.

DON'T BE AN INFLUENCER

When your job is defined as being an "influencer", you may get people to do things differently but you will never be credited – or rewarded – for it. And you will not be able to assess your own progress either.

Try this. Go to LinkedIN (or to any other job searching website of your preference). Enter your criteria and see what opportunities are found and recommended to you.

I bet you will get: fuzzy job descriptions (especially if the job is promoted through a professional recruiter), vague role and responsibility definition, unclear metrics. Salary range will be indicated as meaninglessly as "6 digits OTE" or "competitive package".

But when you look at the job requirements, you will find a lot of details: languages, master degrees, certifications, years of experience, ability to write with your feet and clairvoyance (all right, I made some of those up...).

The latest fad I noticed is the trend of describing the candidate's role as "acting as an influencer" to a more or less defined number of people, functions and areas.

Let me tell you right away: in my experience, to have a job defined as "being an influencer" plainly sucks. It's the least rewarding kind of corporate job ever (and I should know...).

For a start, requiring somebody to be an influencer is a thin disguise for really saying: "look, we could not give you the hierarchical responsibility, the money and the empowerment to really change things around here, so you're stuck with the influencer thing."

In addition, such a role usually does not entail a clear and univocal definition of the operational perimeter, of what to do and how to measure the outcome.

In practice. If you influence a certain behaviour, and the person changes because of you and goes on to achieve something important, you will not be rewarded. As honest as the other person can be, she will not grant you kudos for changing her approach. Sure, you might get a thank you note and a warm feeling inside, but that's all you're gonna get for your effort. This is called corporate ruthlessness.

Conversely, if the other person does not change her behaviour notwithstanding all your attempts (i.e. doesn't buy into your recommendations or does it only partially) then you have wasted everybody's time. And on top of that, if you are passionate about what you do, you will also have had a pretty frustrating experience.

Oh and by the way, how should you assess an influencer? Do you look at how hard he's trying to influence? Or do you factor-in the changed behaviour of people and teams that he influenced? A mix of both? And what metrics do you use? Do you measure how many times he disagreed with a certain way of doing things and count that as "influencing activities"?

Reality is, at the end of the day there can be no hard metrics for influencers. The very nature of the job and the way that it's usually set up in a large company are making it impossible to define those. The annoying consequence of a lack of metrics is that you have no way to improve at what you do, and you've got no quantitative basis to claim your rewards either.

Because of such an unfortunate state of things, the performance evaluation of an influencer can only be carried out based on qualitative feedbacks from managers, peers and colleagues. No hard data. Not good enough I think.

So please be careful next time you look at a job opportunity or to a new position. Avoid anything that sounds as fishy and unrewarding as "being an influencer".

Unless of course you are the big boss, in which case influencing others is really all you should do. That's called leadership, by the way.

BUSINESS, METAPHORS AND ROLE MODELS

Metaphors and role models can be very powerful and help convey what we really mean in a fast and effective way. They are also handy when lacking tangible examples for "showing" what we tell.

In business, it has become common practice to use metaphors. It's generally effective and often fun too. Some of them, however, are definitely abused. The most common one is perhaps sailing, typically used as an example of teamwork. Choose the best course to a destination (i.e. select your target), combat capricious winds (lurking competitors), sail on through unpredictable weather (changing needs of clients) and cross treacherous oceans (economy slow downs).

Formula 1 racing is another popular one, once again used to depict teamwork in high-tech and highly-competitive top performance challenges. For products, it is often the case of quoting a car manufacturer of choice to trace a parallel between just-in-time or lean-production (both of course Toyota's innovations: for an intriguing deep dive on the car manufacturing world, I strongly recommend the book "The machine that changed the world" by James P. Womack, Daniel T. Jones and Daniel Roos), and the best way to innovate in the areas of design and product development.

For leadership attitude and behaviour, Sun Tzu's "The Art of War" is quite simply the industry standard!

Beyond metaphors, I also quite like it when famous historical characters and their accomplishments are used to convey a certain intent, a desired attitude or simply to provide a real-life example of a model to follow.

When talking about creative work, of course a much adopted role model is Leonardo da Vinci, universally considered a genius in many different fields: drawing, painting, civil and military engineering, fashion, music, architecture, sculpture, and many more.

Nonetheless, I personally think that Leonardo is kind of overrated – at least when mentioned as the ultimate example of mastery.

As often happens, when covering larger than life characters biographers can get carried away by the myth and involuntarily neglect historical facts (note: the best biography I have read of Da Vinci is "Leonardo da Vinci – The flights of the mind" by Charles Nicholl – highly recommended).

Leonardo was certainly an outstanding figure in middle ages' Italy and Europe. His curiosity and power of observation, joined with an innate gift to represent reality in drawing, painting, sculpturing and writing, was the real key asset he was born with, and that he managed to develop until the very end.

However he was also a constant tinkerer, who would not hesitate to try new materials or techniques but would thus jeopardise the final results (e.g. The Last Supper), and who would bore quickly of whatever endeavour he was embarking on, to the point of often taking upfront money for work only to promptly move on to the next challenge before finishing the assignment. Testimony of his anxiety is the well documented fact that almost all of his works – including the world famous Mona Lisa – are unfinished.

Without denying Leonardo's greatness for a single moment, I simply believe we cannot really use him as a role model for business purposes.

In my view, a much more relevant figure of creative arts and mastery, this time based on a practical, responsible attitude aimed at innovating and improving his field of expertise, would be Leon Battista Alberti – the original "Universal Man".

Born in Genoa in 1404, Alberti was an author, poet, linguist, architect, philosopher, cryptographer, renaissance humanist and a polymath.

In 1435 he famously authored the book "De Pictura", the first and most famous treatise about the three core rules of painting: perspective, composition and colour.

It's intriguing how he wasn't the first one to identify and focus on those rules, and certainly did not invent them – curiously enough, he wasn't an established painter either!

But he was the first to write about those three elements in a cohesive, convincing and logical way, changing painting forever after. He wrote "De Pictura" in Latin first, but he soon translated it into Italian, having identified this as an opportunity to broaden circulation.

Alberti's rules of painting are perfect for tracing a parallel with the business world.

Rule #1: Perspective.
Analyse the whole picture, focus on details and the broader representation. Control matter in space using a grid/net to locate objects in space.

What it means for business:
- ◦ Look at things from a new, unfamiliar, uncomfortable point of view. Pay attention to how they relate to each other. Understand that what happens on the market never happens in a vacuum, but it always has identifiable causes and effects.

What it delivers:
- ◦ A clearer understanding of the market and its scenarios, players, opportunities and threats.
- ◦ A list of actionable do's and (more importantly) don'ts.
- ◦ A sharper focus on client's needs in relation to your business portfolio of products and services.

Rule #2: Composition.
Decide what subjects will be in your painting, and what is left out.

What it means for business:
- ◦ Help choose what are the best offerings/solutions for the target market/clients. What your company chooses not to do qualifies what you do-do.

What it delivers:
- ◦ A list of priority offerings/solutions.
- ◦ A clearly identified priority target clients.

- A way to decide where to invest and develop and where to cease and desist.

Rule #3: Colour.

Pay attention to both light and shade. Shine a light on important things, shade others that are less important to your painting.

What it means for business:

- Focus on clients, market and opportunities where your company can deliver a winning proposition. If you cannot solve a problem, provide innovation or deliver better value for money, don't get involved. If there are areas where all you can provide is "industry average" goods, just move on quickly and focus the attention on your shining silver bullets. Colour them bright, paint them with the boldest strokes of your brush so that everybody will pay attention.

What it delivers:

- Value proposition statements that resonate internally – your employees and partners – and externally – the market and your clients.
- Sharp, relevant and to-the-point marketing and sales deliverables.
- Tangible, measurable benefits easy to identify and purchase.

This is just an example on how we can draw inspiration from great people of the past. I hope it shows how quite straightforward, and fun it can be to link their experience and teachings to our modern day business behaviours and needs. I'm sure you can come up with more.

SETTING THE RIGHT EXPECTATIONS

Setting and regularly reviewing expectations drives behaviour, that's the reason why I believe it's the single most important task of a manager's job. Unbelievable as it may sound though, a lot of managers fail to actually understand how important this task is. I've had the misfortune of working with a few of those: they try to ignore it, pay lip service to it or skip it altogether.

Granted, setting clear expectations is never easy. It takes time and it requires analytical skills as well as an uncanny ability to appreciate the bigger picture. You need to make sure that your team members have matching but also individual objectives to work toward, and more importantly that all of those fit together. Pretty much like pieces of a puzzle reveal the full photograph, matching expectations should paint the strategic direction of your business.

I like to think of expectations along three main areas:

1. **Business expectations**: this is where a manager defines and shares the business imperatives plus the high level objectives. Objectives are of course different from expectations. They should always be quantitative - e.g. $$$ of revenue target, % increase of profit. Expectations are built upon objectives, and are a mix of quantitative and qualitative elements. Everybody on the team should be clear about what they will endeavour to achieve, what the key activities will be and which metrics and measures will be adopted.

2. **Behaviour expectations**: this is where the rules for working together are laid out. Things like sharing information freely, regularly reporting progress on main business projects, but also the establishment of a healthy life-work balance (e.g. agreed working hours, no emails on weekends).

3. **Principles expectations**: this is where the team agrees on what core values it believes in. Openness, respect, trust. If done in the right way, setting the right principles will build up a sense of belonging that will make the team work with each other (versus just working together) toward a common goal.

As said, the time needed and the difficulty of performing the task is certainly one of the reasons why some managers don't seem to bother.

Another reason, also quite common, is that some managers don't actually set clear and demanding expectations for themselves to start with! That's plainly wrong and unacceptable.

In management, one needs to consider what I define a "triad model", in which setting expectations is – arguably – the most important element alongside:

a) defining clear objectives and
b) devising straightforward metrics.

The simplest action you can undertake as an employee is to demand to have clear, simple and written objectives and expectations. Ask your manager to set aside the right amount of time and energy to complete the exercise early on in the fiscal year.

The second step is then to make sure that performance against expectations is assessed and reviewed regularly. In no way is a simple yearly assessment sufficient. I would argue that even a quarterly one would not be enough. Managers should make every possible effort to perform some of these assessment in person, as the exercise really increases in difficulty over the phone.

To help and facilitate these regular assessments, managers need to foster and develop a culture of using simple and straightforward action trackers. These basic tools represent the elementary building blocks toward implementing an execution driven team. And in turn they will make much easier to set your expectations.

I hope these simple steps will help managers understand and appreciate the importance of properly managing expectations. Failure to do so will make managers weak, cause their teams to under-perform and in general instigate biased behaviours. Ultimately it will damage the company and the manager itself. But doing it right will definitely improve employee performance, fulfilment and ultimately retention.

FOCUS V. TUNNEL VISION

The business focus on enterprises is usually on what's directly ahead. After all, we are all consistently told that to succeed at something you have to focus. Sportsmen call it "being in the zone", and the general consensus is that focus equals good.

The risk of focusing so much though is that you might develop a lack of peripheral vision, or so called tunnel vision.

You see, focus is a strange thing. Think of cameras: before the auto-focus feature was invented – now of course pretty much standardly used across amateurs and professionals – every user had the choice of selecting which part of the picture would be in focus. Sure, this led to any number of crappy snapshots we're all familiar with, the ones where the worthless tree in the background is perfectly sharp whilst the main subject in the foreground is blurred beyond recognition.

But it also gave the power of choice. Agree, auto-focus does too but it doesn't really provide the same degree of flexibility and of potential, creative failure. Keen photographers of course might jump in at this stage and mention the revolutionary Lytro camera that takes pictures and allows the user to bring into focus whatever area at a later stage. That's a feature that would be very handy in the business world too!

Anyway, here's why I think both focus and the related depth-of-field are relevant to better business practices. In short, I believe that when focusing too much you run the very real risk of missing out important details on the periphery of whatever subject you are working on, and of lacking the necessary depth-of-field to sharpen your business snapshot.
What happens is that you develop tunnel vision.

Think about driving a vehicle. Everybody knows that you must focus on what's ahead on the road. At the same time, though, you also need to check your side-view and rear-view mirrors regularly, as well as get an appreciation of what the other drivers, pedestrians and general traffic are doing all around you. And naturally you have to adjust your speed to make sure that the projected trajectory of your car is not going to collide with other vehicles or objects.

Likewise, at work it's good to look ahead and concentrate on one thing at a time, but you should make sure you never neglect paying attention to what's going on around you. In fact, that's exactly where most of the interesting or disrupting things usually happen. Focus is required because through focus you make sure you give all your attention and best effort to the task at hand – big or small. But you need to make sure that by focusing you don't overlook or miss the big picture. In other words, unless you put what you are doing in the broader context, you run the risk of being misled into doing something that might become detrimental to some other task, activity or initiative.

So can you or should you always start a discussion or an activity being 100% focused? I think you should not. I believe that you need to start by getting a general appreciation for what's going on: players, extended ecosystem, changing priorities at play and the general dynamics of the business.

If you start being completely focused, you may miss indicators that if picked up early enough will actually make you focus better at a later stage, and improve the outcome of what you do.

Horses that wear blinkers will not stray from the established path or direction, but they become defenceless to attacks coming from other directions. Being a prey by nature, a horse forcefully focused on what's ahead will actually be more vulnerable to predators. In other words, focus can mark the difference between life and death.

Finally, focusing too much or too early can also cause anxiety because it makes it easier for others to take you by surprise. Life, and business life particularly, is tough, and there are so many concurrent things happening at the same time, with a very real potential impact on our actions and decisions, that we simply cannot afford to be too much focused on one thing at a time.

Learn from nature and from life: look at the game-changing information at the periphery of your view and make sure you focus only after taking in all the "light" through your personal lens.

HOW TO MAKE BETTER USE OF YOUR TIME

Technology advancements are supposed to make our business life easier right? Well, that's the idea but reality is that most of us are constantly interrupted by all sorts of different distractions.

I'm a very organized person, and I do layout my days and weeks in a strongly structured way. It might look a little bit paranoid at first, but if you check out my schedule you won't find much wasted time. So to protect what I consider a "very best practice", I have developed a simple dashboard that I use to indicate to people what to expect when trying to reach me.

For each of the listed channels, I developed a set of policies to protect my day from intrusions and time-wasters.

SMART PHONE: voice calls.

If I don't recognize the number on the display, I won't answer the phone. If the caller id is hidden, I won't answer the call. If I'm busy doing something else which I deem important, I won't answer the call.

SMART PHONE: text messages (SMS), IM.

I read SMS and IM messages pretty much in real time, even if I don't recognize the sender. However I almost never reply in real time unless it's some personal message or emergency. At work I've used mainly Microsoft Outlook and Lync, but I don't synchronize the status between the twos. I believe this setup provides more flexibility: should I move some Outlook Calendar meetings during the day I don't have to worry about Lync accurately reflecting the change (and sometimes it just doesn't).

I always set my IM status as busy, but I usually reply pretty quick if you ask me nicely, even if I'm busy doing something else. Way faster than a lot of people I know that are "available" on IM all the time, anyway...

EMAIL

Contrary to popular corporate belief, email is not a real time tool. Hence I don't do real time emails.

I download emails three/four times per day from the server to my PC, then I just set Outlook to offline. I sort them by sender, topic and date, and then I work my way through. I usually have next to zero unread emails from one week to the next. I do use fast reading and skim-reading, and I file by sender and by organization. I used to file email by topic too, but I found that it's much easier for me to remember who sent me something rather than remembering the subject.

So how do you wrap up all of the above practices into a sensible approach that makes the best use of your time? Here's one of my typical work days you can use as a template.

7 am: morning shower/shave: think about something creative. (e.g. how to do specific jobs or tasks differently, how the team could work in an innovative way). Usually high level big picture stuff to get my brain going.

Breakfast: read online news (RSS based) for 10 minutes, occasionally tweet interesting stuff if you find any.

Office (home): first thing in the morning, spend 30 minutes to download, check, sort and prioritize emails. Reply to any email that is really urgent (remember, that's urgent according to your judgment, not others). Look at your schedule and go through the list of tasks you set yourself for the day:

- Long/difficult/articulated tasks = max 2 per day
- Short/simple tasks = max 2 in the morning + 2 in the afternoon.

Take phone calls only if the caller is someone you know won't waste your time, otherwise engage voice mail and sort at lunch time.

12 pm: Download/check email again, re-sort and re-prioritize. Reply to urgent ones.

1 pm: lunch break - 30 minutes for food, 15 minutes for brief walk whilst sorting voice mail, 15 minutes for thinking.

2 pm: spend 30 minutes to think about big picture things (refreshing early morning pondering or new ones). Call back people who left voice mail, go through the list of tasks for the rest of the day. Anytime it feels right, take a short 10 minute nap.

6 pm: download/check email again, sort and re-prioritize. Check voice mail again. Go home (i.e. shut home office door).

Evening: dinner and quality time with family, occasional trip to shops (not often!).

Night: rework and finalize task list for next day. Occasionally download/check email again. Sort, prioritize, answer urgent ones.

10.30 pm: read, stream and watch film or sport event.

12 am: bed time.

As you can see there are no secrets or magic shortcuts to make time, just establish a solid schedule and adopt enough discipline to stick to tasks and practices. What do you think, could it work for you too?

ASK THE RIGHT QUESTIONS

Here we go again: new team, new team building exercise. Open questions time is a classic, you know the format: any question goes, let's be open and transparent to each other.

I'm sure you have been through this exercise at least once in your professional life. It is certainly an interesting one, that if done correctly can indeed bring a lot of clarity and foster a better team understanding, setup and development.

My experience however is that because of the way the exercise is usually setup, the participants tend to almost naturally ask the "wrong" questions. Let me elaborate with a quick example of what I mean.

A new team is formed. The new boss sends out some material depicting at some level the team's scope, responsibility, duties and objectives. For hi- tech companies usually a lot of jargon is used, and for large companies there's usually a degree of organizational complexity that contributes to blur things.

Then people are invited to a meeting where more information will be shared, and they are required to think of some good 'open questions' to raise in the meeting.

What I've regularly seen happen then, over and over again, is that almost all of the participants ask very detailed questions: sometime around specific tasks, sometime on operational processes to be developed, used or refined, sometimes even on tools and technology pieces to be called into play.

All very relevant and useful questions for sure, however the objective of the exercise is somehow missed. Why?

1. Because people stick to their comfort zone. They are not used to looking above and beyond, deep and broad. They stick to what they "know".
2. Because they show a natural resistance to openness. People are afraid to be open and transparent. The reason is simple: when you are open and transparent, you are just yourself. And being yourself does not mean that people will like you, or even agree with you. Western civilization has taught us that acceptance is everything, even more so in a business situation. So people are afraid to speak their mind, and to show their real nature. "What if the boss disagrees?" "What if I disagree with the boss, should I tell her?".

The duty of a good manager – or a good leader rather – is to tear these barriers down, make people look at the destination and ask the right questions on how to get there.

Even simple exercises as the one above can be extremely valuable in teaching to open up in a true way, thus benefitting both the management team, the employees and the ultimately the company itself.

So next time it's "open question" time, let go and be yourself. Ask what you really want to ask, push the limits, create some disruption. Your team will be better off for that.

7. BREAKING YOUR OWN RULES

Consensus is the business of politics. (M. Crichton)

It's good to be organised and to have clarity on processes and procedures. Simple things like building lists and regularly ticking off completed tasks not only provide a record of activities for you to reflect on, but also build a sense of achievement at the end of the day, no matter if the tasks were big or small.

Rules, even those that you have built yourself to achieve increased efficiency and productivity, can however become too restrictive and rigid at times, and ultimately slow you down.

So, what to do? Simple: make it a habit to break them. No, I'm not encouraging you to mess up your life and throw every certainty away.

What I actually recommend is that you consciously and deliberately look at some of the things you routinely do and break them. Change perspective on situations. Look at problems from different angles. For example, immediately trying to seek a solution to a problem might sometimes be the wrong approach, much better to break the issue down in elementary building blocks and then analyze those to check whether they really represent a problem.

Challenge yourself and ask "can I perform this specific task in a different way"?

A good example for explaining this approach are musicians.

Professional musicians play and compose music. Sometimes they play somebody else's music, and that's fine because they interpret that particular composition through their own abilities and sensibility. Mostly they create songs, and in this case they express even further their inner feelings and emotions, by translating those into musical notes and lyrics.

Do they always perform those songs in the same way? Of course not. The chord sequence, for example, might be the same, but the player may alternate different chord formations or play them on different positions on the piano keyboard or guitar neck.

The melody might sound fundamentally similar, but the performer might add a few subtle changes here and there to reflect her specific feelings at the time of the performance. By introducing similar subtle changes in the way you work, you will discover new ways of doing things, and also avoid fatigue from mindless repetition.

Give it a try, play it again Sam, only slightly differently this time.

15 REASONS WHY YOU ARE FAILING TO INNOVATE

In my experience, the following are the 15 most common reasons for companies to fail:

1. Your company is afraid of taking risks (a.k.a. you are not bold enough).
2. You don't ask why often enough.
3. You listen to the same old sources (for example, nobody believes IT market analysts anymore – mostly they have no clue and/or are on the payroll of the big companies).
4. You play a new game by the old rules.
5. You think too small.
6. You think too long term.
7. You're stuck on strategy (instead of getting into execution as fast as you can).
8. You are afraid of conflicts.
9. You do not listen hard enough.
10. You don't speak simple enough (essentially that's why nobody understands you).
11. You pay too much attention to what your competitors do.
12. You are too naive (i.e. believe everything you are told).
13. You are not uncomfortable enough in your job (hence you cannot feel the need to innovate).
14. You are surrounded by people who suck up to you (or pay lip service), believe what makes you/your team/your company look good and/or is convenient for you.
15. You are not cynical enough (just in case you haven't noticed: the business world is cynical).

GIVE IT FOR FREE

In the IT outsourcing business, a popular technique for service providers is to approach clients and prospects through so called "consultancy services". These usually have the format of short one day fairly free-flowing brainstorming sessions, where so-called subject matter experts take the prospect through a number of topics, usually in relation to IT transformation (infrastructure, application, service management) or, lately, envisioning a move to the cloud.

These sessions require a solid preparation on both sides, and are usually quite expensive, anything from $20k up to hundreds of thousands of dollars.

Sales teams typically try to charge the client, maybe agreeing to detract the consultancy cost if future business is granted. Often the sales team picks up the bill and it ends up as a sales cost.

Of course, giving consultancy activities away for free is frowned upon by most sales managers, right? The consensus here is that something "free" does not have a perceived value attached to it.

On the other hand, even charging those consultancy days is no guarantee of future business, as clients can enjoy a full assessment and then take the recommendations to one of your competitors for implementing the solution.

So free v. not-free becomes one of the many catch-22 situations that business presents at every other turn.

Let me be clear: I'm a big fan of free stuff. If you've paid attention to the consumer world lately, the last few years have seen a major growth of free goodies, in the form of e-books, white papers, complimentary event tickets, and the sorts.

As Chris Anderson, editor in chief of Wired magazine, has expertly articulated in his book "Free: the future of a radical price" (a book that is not for free unfortunately!), there is a definite rise of new pricing models that give products and services to customers for free, with the intent to make them "touch" and experience before buying. I can see no reason why this trend should be restricted to consumers only.

If we go back to the example, how should consultancy services be sold then?

Fundamentally, you, as a service provider, should enter the session with a well formed (and informed) point of view. Gone are the "white sheet" days, when sales reps were there to note down the clients' requests.

The degree and thoroughness of your homework will enable you to actively drive the discussion and make the client pay attention. Your objective is for every word you say to resonate loud and clear.

Take a bold approach. The majority of enterprise clients might know what they want, but don't necessarily know what their business needs are.

It's your duty to make them understand what it is that they need, and then convince them that your company is the one best positioned to deliver it. In other words, modern clients have to be taught.

Let's look at a simple example, and take the fashionable cloud proposition. Here's an approach I favour (simplified):

"Dear client, based on our understanding of your business model, your IT core capabilities and your industry trends, we think you simply cannot ignore the cloud proposition. If you do, this is going to happen:

- Your ageing apps will degrade in performance in time, seriously impact your productivity, and sooner or later cause your operations to stop altogether
- costly maintenance of your current IT environment will limit your ability to invest in new technologies
- ageing technology will open your information platform to security threats and costly liabilities
- You will keep paying for resources that your company does not use (or under uses)
- You will be unable to drive your company's growth and business expansion

Now, would you like to have a look at how my company can help you avoid all of the above?"

Let's be honest: how many account managers do you know who are able to do just that? Actually, by not charging the client, you'll be in a better position to be bold and upfront.

It's almost like you have no real vested interest whether the client is finding the service valuable – hence agrees to be charged for it – or not. You are there because you care about that potential client. And if you care, you don't charge upfront, but invest your time and make the best effort.

The question now becomes: "How can sales be incented to take this route?". After all, if there is no sale, there's no commission right?

Well, unfortunately the perfect carrot does not exist. Purely financial incentives are dangerous, as we know, because they might encourage short cuts and myopic sales (i.e. one company division selling to the detriment of another). Non-financial incentives are interesting but difficult to conceive: dinners for two, paid weekend trips, etcetera might be fun in the beginning but may not stand the test of time. Rather than trying to find the perfect incentive mix, I think that sales leaders should foster a culture where sales reps understand that not everything they do is subject to incentives.

A sound sales compensation plan, defined and agreed at the beginning of the year, should reward financial achievements - hard metrics - and desired behaviour - soft metrics. Once defined, it should be left alone for the rest of the fiscal year, as additional incentives, even if devised with the best intentions, will only generate confusion, anxiety, and ultimately actually defocus the overall sales effort.

The time is ripe for a radical change in the way we sell products and services to enterprise-class clients: be bold, give something away for free, show that you care, reward results and attitude.

IP ANYONE?

I have spent many years working in information technology. When I started, more than thirty years ago, it was all about super-cool hardware - fault tolerant computing for example, or hot swappable disk drives - and accelerated development of enterprise class software programs.

Across the years, through an ever shortening cycle of technological innovation, the "coolness" of working in IT slowly but progressively declined. The recent trend of IT "consumerization" fundamentally transformed information technology into something you just use when needed and then forget about it. A decreased perception of IT value, in turn, caused a pricing war and consequently declining margins for those companies providing IT products and services, which tried to tackle their business problems, for instance, through the acquisition of new competencies and skills by merging with other key market players, looking for more efficient scale and coverage.

Unfortunately, it's a game of trial and error. Many large corporations are still trying to make sense of what shape and format they should assume in the future to have a chance at growth and success. It's like everybody knows the general direction, but nobody really knows the destination.

In particular, corporate acquisitions – often very expensive ones – seem to over promise and under deliver.

Augmentation of competencies and skills that are supposed to integrate existing ones or open up a whole new world of opportunities in terms of product development and market coverage, very often turn into wishful thinking. To me, many of these acquisitions resemble nothing more than desperate shortcuts to acquire intellectual property that:

1. the company is unable to develop internally through their R&D or Labs because of lack

of focus, processes, infrastructure, innovation engine.

2. the company would be able to develop internally but that would require too much time or too much money to be invested.

The acquired intellectual property, potentially key factor for the development and positioning of a renewed offering, largely sits ill integrated with the existing product and service portfolio, and usually fails to produce any tangible financial or commercial benefit.

After all, if you are an acquirable company with a desirable IP and/or product that gets swallowed by a larger corporation, a few things usually happen:

1. the acquiring company's management boldly declares that the "strategic" move will be providing years of revenues and market share growth.
2. the acquired company's management enthusiastically states that they will finally have access to key resources and be able to scale their mind-blowing technology and conquer the world.
3. everybody tries very hard for the first few months to convince each other and everybody else that it will work.

Then, usually within a year or so from the acquisition, reality strikes:

1. most of the acquired company's leadership team leaves, considerably richer (in hard currency or stock options) and looking for new and innovative business challenges.

2. the acquiring company either does not have a clue on how to integrate the new technology into their products or things have moved on, market wise, anyway. This is when the management quietly decides that the technology wasn't so world-changing after all.
3. everybody goes back to business as if nothing happened.

At least in the old days companies used to be acquired because of their customer base or because of their market share, maybe because of their financial strength or some very specific patent.

But today, it seems to me that more and more we are putting on a show, which is just that – for show.

The rate of innovation and technology adoption is so fast that for a large corporation it's almost impossible to be able to build rapidly and solidly enough the knowledge and competencies needed to win in the market by playing what I call "catching up by shopping around".

What we need are more visionary and game changing companies that not only accept risk but embrace it and are willing to replace old behaviours, whilst they still work, with new innovative ones.

I know it sounds like a dangerous proposition, and in fact the majority of established large companies are historically risk averse, discouraging any particularly disruptive initiative at any level.

After all, for the average employee is much easier to say yes and fit in than to be a contrarian and make the effort to look at things from a different perspective.

Whilst it's true that change can happen by itself, it's also a fact that it can be accelerated significantly if the right business triggers are recognised, understood and shared through the organisation. The trick is to foster a culture of developing those triggers by investing in people and infrastructure, and to focus on producing in-house intellectual property that will set your company apart and ultimately drive its growth and success.

THE SOUL OF A COMPANY

Companies are mostly the expression of their founder's values and beliefs. As they grow and acquire other companies, those very values are diluted and are inevitably lost along the way. Is there a way to avoid it?

I think the phenomenon is well known. Pretty much all companies, at the very beginning, are a reflection of what the founders believe and want to achieve. The large majority of entrepreneurs do not set out to make an awful lot of money – believe it or not they start their enterprise for different reasons. Money is mostly just a (very nice) byproduct.

Special companies have special values, in which early stage employees also believe and reflect themselves. In turn, those "core" employees foster those values and pass them to the newcomers, who in time make them grow too. This is where employees really care about the company: not because they get paid to, but because they feel it's their company too. There is a very strong feeling of belonging and identification: we stand for the same things.

As those special enterprises grow, very often they go through acquisitions of other businesses, being competitors or simply side business to complete their portfolio. Inevitably, these acquisitions bring in different kinds of employees, who themselves maybe believed in an altogether different set of company values, which attracted them to their original firm.

Through a few of these mergers or acquisitions, the company leadership and management usually changes, becoming – in the best of cases – a mix of the previous ones with the newcomers.

Result: original values and beliefs are diluted, often even destroyed after a few of these cycles. The soul of the company is gone.

At this stage, one is led to think about the inevitability of all that. After all, economies and markets change all the time, so should companies operating in those economies and markets.

However, I believe that the destruction of what I call the "founding fathers credo" is the main reason why great companies turn into mediocre ones. Throughout pretty much all of my working life, I have had the good fortune of being able to choose which company to work for and it's a special feeling to know that likewise the companies that hired me also chose me among others.

When a company merges or acquires another one, where is the personal choosing?

In fact, it's actually almost always the case that the whole leadership team of the acquired company leaves after a short while, and

I would argue that on top of the obvious advantageous economic terms, the real reason is that they were not chosen and did not choose the values and beliefs of the other company. Companies merge and acquire others because of market economy rules, not because of value fitting or soul-matching. Don't believe who tells you otherwise. Companies however are not only made of processes and products, costs and revenues. They are made of people, and if people do not believe in the company, they will not care. A company where employees do not care will always and utterly fail.

WORKING TOGETHER OR WITH EACH OTHER?

How many times have you heard the statement "... and for this position we are really looking for a strong team player..." or "...my best skill is being able to work well within a team of ...."?

Well, I for one have heard this refrain a thousand times, but in my experience I almost always discovered it to be either an empty statement or plain wishful thinking.
What I couldn't help but notice is that most people mistake "working together" with "working with each other".

Working together often means reporting to the same boss, sharing some org chart function (or just plainly the same cubicle) or having some broadly defined common objectives.

Being polite, politically correct and saying a lot of "thank you" and "I'm sorry" is another typical trait, just like closing an eye on missed deadlines or sub-par contents.

But you know what? I truly believe that working with each other is what really counts.

Doing work that matters not only for your specific tasks but also to help, enable or get another team member going. Committing clearly and delivering on time – not once, but always. Telling your colleague that "no, that piece of work is not good enough", and lending a hand to improve it. Showing up on time at meetings, sending timely meeting notes, logging action items and reviewing them regularly. Setting tough objectives for you and the other teammates. Doing something for nothing, not just because you are told to or because you want to impress your boss, but to actually build something of value with and for each other.

Working with each other means understanding yours and the other's strengths and building those into an outstanding cooperation. It means saying no a lot, and yes a few times, but really meaning it. Give credit where it belongs, but share freely your most valuable work and make it available to your team members.

Share. Teach. Give. Respect. Grow. These are the reasons why you should work with each other.

8. LEADING YOUR PACK

In my work experience I have only rarely encountered real leaders, and the main reason why, I think, is that to be a leader is really hard work.

A leader has to match her personal brilliance with curiosity, focus and drive to take initiative. Has to develop a way to get people to take action not because they are commanded to but because they want to. Leaders are foremost teachers who are not afraid to keep learning. Anybody can develop those qualities. Not everybody is determined enough to put in the hard work too.

Human beings need a purpose to motivate them and confidence to move them forward. Build your team's skills and capabilities to produce quality results. Agitate things if needs be, but always keep in mind that your main goal is to teach.

So are you ready to lead your pack?

HOW TO MOVE ON

For many of us, it is difficult to move on, even when we decide to change jobs or to get new assignments and responsibilities. We might be in a position where we really like what we do but realise that it's time to change, still somehow we tend to remain anchored to the comfortable feelings and emotions of our previous role.

Fortunately, you can learn to let go, forget about the past and concentrate on the future.

What you need to do is to push yourself out of the comfort zone; in fact, I bet in your current job you are probably feeling safe. You have the skills to perform it in the best possible way, you master the tools, you have built a network of colleagues, partners and clients who trust you, and you feel comfortable and professionally proficient.

Conversely, a new job or position brings in excitement, the opportunity to meet and network with new colleagues and the chance to tackle new challenges, but also a lot of unknown, potential discomfort or even pain (at least in the beginning).

Changing jobs is ultimately about learning something new and about giving yourself a new set of demanding objectives.

The best way to prepare for that, is to take the time to mentally disconnect from your previous job, as I believe that brain fatigue is almost as bad as physical tiredness, and unfortunately it cannot be replenished as easily.

In most cases, taking on a new responsibility or joining a new company requires a fresh mind approach, and we all know how difficult it is to do so when you have been up until yesterday involved in demanding and intensive work assignments and responsibilities.

The switch works best if you have the good fortune to have some colleague to hand your old job to.

Try to apply some common sense techniques: if you are staying on at the same company, resist keeping your name in the old distribution lists, for example.

Do not tell your colleagues that you will always be available to consult or provide a point of view – because you know that you will immerse yourself in your new role from day one.

I'm not suggesting you should burn all your bridges, but certainly that you should let less people cross them to get to you. Be ruthlessly selective.

From a practical stand point, try to tie up all the loose ends by your last day in the job, for example:

- back up and delete all the emails directly linked to your previous job. People will ask you about old stuff or communications, this way you can bounce them back easily.
- backup and delete from your laptop all the marketing materials: documents, slide decks, videos, promotional brochures; store and delete all sales plans, client data, pipeline information.
- if allowed, add to your email address an indication of your new job (e.g. john.d@acme.com - direct sales)

Ultimately, moving on is about developing yourself so make sure you are setting aside enough time, focus and energy to achieve just that.

A TIME AND PLACE FOR BEING CREATIVE

When is the best time to be creative? There's probably no standard answer, since we all might have our own little formulas and scenarios.

Like a lot of creative people I know, I usually find it easier to write posts and articles when I'm not at home, when I'm traveling for business or when I really have little time to do it properly.

I haven't figured out exactly why that's the case, but I suppose that part of the reason is that being out of a familiar situation, place or routine helps me take a fresh perspective on things.

Intriguingly, this need for a certain degree of mild discomfort applies to music as well. As any serious musician would confirm, it's incredibly difficult to perform when you are feeling happy with the world. It's tough to play the blues when your life is great, for example, and in fact great blues musicians had very tough lives.

It's interesting then to notice that as human beings, maybe we really need to have a certain amount of tension – for lack of a better definition – in our life if we want to drive and take on creative activities, initiatives and projects.

Little things that make your legs shake before speaking at a big convention, or knot your stomach when looking down at the audience when performing on stage.

At the work place people often shy away from tension, believing that it will only disrupt the assumed – and mostly fictitious – harmony represented by conventional politeness and politically correct exchanges.

A classic example is the meeting where everybody knows that a new and sometimes radical approach at doing things differently is needed, but nobody has the courage to push too much for fear of hurting somebody else's feelings.

Personally, I have actually been told more than once that at times I do that quite well: being direct, shaking people by the shoulders (metaphorically, of course!) and just plainly building up some strong emotional response from the participants.

I believe that creativity feeds on controversy, on out of the norm behaviours and the ability to see things differently. You cannot be really creative unless you break something, so to speak. A creative tension is the perfect driver to do that, even if it means stepping on people's toes and disrupting their world.

So a few practical suggestions: don't structure your creative routine too much, seek (or artificially create) a little discomfort and leverage that as a creative spark, and most importantly never be too complacent, with yourself and with others.

After all, when everybody agrees on something, it's often a sign that the limits have not been pushed hard enough.

HOW TO MAKE YOURSELF REDUNDANT

If you want to have a better chance at advancing your career, you should try very hard to make yourself redundant.

In terms of career development, it's obviously good practice to plan your next steps well in advance. As a general rule, I think you should avoid feeling too comfortable in your current job, and regularly assess what would happen if your function was to suddenly disappear from the organizational chart.

Consider also that the worst thing that can happen to your professional life is to become irrelevant, right? Doesn't really matter if you are managing a team or if you are an individual contributor, the moment you feel like you are not adding value anymore, it's too late for your career.

I know it might seem like a suicidal proposition, but I believe that you should aim at doing your job so well, that at a certain point you will not be needed anymore.

Say you have a specific task to accomplish. For example, to get a newly formed team to understand their role, responsibility and expected contribution. Once that level of proficiency is achieved, your job is done. There is no need to hang around and keep holding hands. Move on, seek and get a new challenge.

Similarly, when there are many organizational changes, you might be in a position where you feel stuck in-between organizations and charters. Make sure you honestly assess your results against the objectives you were given, share a detailed report to document how you met them, and demand to look at other opportunities.

Great professionals deliver and move on. Don't do this to show how important or how good you are. Do it to rationally show how well you performed your duties, and do it to highlight how the world would still go on even when you're gone.

This technique, apart from keeping you honest, also helps you feel "on the edge", to combat the apathy that a comfortable job can bring. This way, you can be ready to move into positions that will develop your skills and advance your career further, without leaving a problem behind you.

Also consider that in some cases, if you are doing a truly great job, you might never get a chance to move somewhere else: your boss might selfishly feel that losing you would cause too much trouble for the team (and herself), thus de-facto building a wall around you.

Don't let anybody ever take you for granted, that would be the death of your career (and possibly of your life too).
So the key is to strike a balance between stellar performance and flexibility to move, between relevance and expendability, between static and dynamic, and ultimately between comfort and risk.

The final recommendation of course is to act now: it's never too early to change jobs, but it's almost always too late to do so.

BEWARE OF THE CATALYST

Have you ever been offered a job where your would have "been the catalyst" for something (growth, change, business acceleration)?

It seems that broad job descriptions are becoming the norm these days, especially in large or very large companies. In the old days, it was pretty easy to understand, at least at high level, what your job would be by just looking at the job title. Stuff like "project manager" or "marketing lead" or even "technical supervisor". Nowadays, not only do we get fancy job titles, but job descriptions become weirder too, often with little reference to the "real" duties.

The latest I heard of these craze goes something like this: "you will be acting as the catalyst in a value chain of functions, who will neither report hierarchically nor functionally to you but who will depend on your role to make things seamlessly work".

Now, apart from the obvious nonsense of being responsible for driving the behaviour of people who could not care less about you, who in their sane minds would like to be a catalyst? And even worse, who the hell established that a catalyst is a good business metaphor to be used?

Let's get some help on the definitions: "Catalysis is the change in rate of a chemical reaction due to the participation of a substance called a catalyst." [source: Wikipedia].

So the catalyst does participate in a chemical reaction, either to accelerate it or – surprise surprise – to slow it down. It does that by interacting with the substances that are brought together to form a chemical reaction. So in theory, going back to our business metaphor, a catalyst could add some value to the chemical reaction itself by just being an external factor. But it might as well just slow everything down – kind of a worrying possibility don't you think?

Even more interesting: "Although catalysts are not consumed by the reaction itself, they may be inhibited, deactivated, or destroyed by secondary processes." [source: Wikipedia].

That's also quite interesting. What this means is that even if you do a good job, the best you can hope for is to survive the reaction, or if your luck runs out you might dissolve or evaporate. Not that exciting for your career development...

Finally, and this is a killer in my view: "A catalyst works by providing an alternative reaction pathway to the reaction product."

Basically, it means that the reaction would happen anyway even without the catalyst, by just leaving things to themselves. Or, even better said, a catalyst without a chemical reaction ready to happen is useless.

So back to the business metaphor. If you have identified the need for a certain process or set of processes to happen across a value chain to which multiple functions play, why the heck don't you:

1. make clear to the contributing parties that until they bring the right components the "chemical reaction" won't happen, or
2. empower a controlling external agent to make sure each party does behave as expected.

Bringing in a simple catalyst, that might or might not accelerate things, is not going to guarantee better performance or even a general improvement of things. As we've seen, all it will do is to get the catalyst extremely frustrated – i.e. when there is a lack of components to the solution ready to be "catalysed" – or potentially

destroy the catalyst itself after the reaction
has happened.

Quite an appealing job proposition: an
indication of a job well done equals your
destruction.

9. FOLLOWERS TURNED BELIEVERS

If you are now leading your pack, congratulations. You should be proud of what you achieved. However, keep in mind that with leadership comes a great responsibility, because your followers will sooner or later turn into believers.

They will believe in you, your principle, your work ethics and your objectives. Not because of you, but thanks to you.

It's their belief they express by working under your leadership, but they will always look at you for providing the drive to nurture those beliefs.

Ultimately, always remember that the best leaders deliver the goods or, as I like to say, they ship.

ZEN, LEADERSHIP AND THE CORPORATE WORLD

The corporate world is incredibly complex. It starts at organizational level - matrix teams, dotted line reporting, "glocal" (global and local) coverage - and very quickly spreads to job roles and definitions, then to the product portfolio, to the market coverage and the client segmentation, ending up with all sorts of mix sales channels, models and motions. And I haven't even mentioned the competitors!

It's time to go back to a simpler reference model. If we look at some of the key evangelists of radical simplification and their teachings – like Garr Reynolds or Leo Babauta - we can get some helpful advice in trying to chart a possible approach to such simplification.

One pivotal point is the need to take stuff out of things to make them easy to use and enjoy. Think of all the effort and time (hence cost) you spend trying to sort out who to send a business email to. Or who to invite to the next sales meeting, or product review. Painful, wasteful, not fun.

A second key point is the need to use our beginner's mind more often, so that we can break the "we always did it like this before" syndrome.

The third and final one is the need to foster a feeling of nakedness as full transparency, and be open to critics and suggestions. Forget political power plays, lip service, entrenchment.

Wait a minute: am I oversimplifying things here? Is it that simple to apply these principles to the corporate world?

SIMPLICITY

Quite simply (ah!), I think this concept scares the hell out of practically every manager, director and VP I've known.

Simplicity to them is the biggest threat they can possible face because it equals accountability. If they build a simple presentation, people might actually see through it and understand how full of nothing it is.

If they draft a simple business plan, anybody would be able to see that their assumptions just do not make sense in the majority of the cases (a.k.a. the famous "if we could only get 1% of that huge market" syndrome).

If they talk simply, they fear they might not just be able to convince – or rather confuse – people enough, and end up getting tough and potentially embarrassing questions from the audience.

So they just push back. It cannot be put in one slide instead of ten. I have to list five priorities instead of one.

BEGINNER'S MIND

Just think for a moment at the typical job posting. The very first thing that is required? Job experience. Then it's about knowledge of specific tools, sales experience, industry knowledge, etc.

Now, I know that forward looking managers should hire for fit and not for knowledge, but really how many times have you seen it happen in the corporate world?

So it's hopeless to think that you would be allowed even to pretend not to possess much background knowledge about a subject and be encouraged to build a plan or business proposition – big or small – around it. This would spell failure to the top management, plain and simple waste of time and resources. But actually it's the very key move to make if you are looking for a completely fresh approach to your endeavours.

NAKEDNESS OR TRANSPARENCY

Let me say it plain and loud: nobody in the corporate world is fully transparent. Neither to the outside world – market, clients, competitors, etc. – nor to the internal audience. Everybody will always hide something, twist something else, talk as little as possible of weaknesses or faults and dwell on positive aspects, real or assumed, of whatever they do. For what I know, corporate is actually synonym of opaqueness (of course the natural antonym of transparency).

Telling it all is dangerous at best, and against corporate policy all the time. You can get into big trouble if you are transparent in the business world. I've seen it happen so many times.

SO WHAT DO WE NEED TO DO?

I believe that the above three powerful zen principles of simplicity, beginner's mind and nakedness are completely relevant to the business and corporate world too.

The challenge is to develop some basic but effective techniques to drive those concepts into the corporate world in a way that overcomes the many barriers and no-can-do signs that people will put up in front of you.

Show that simplicity will make people more effective in what they do, measure and quantify how a beginner's approach will help address complex issues, maybe by taking us less time to fix a problem if we pretend it's the first time we look at it.

As a manager, put a premium on transparency and honesty when dealing with colleagues, clients and even competitors, and reward the individuals and teams that excel in doing so.

It will take time but I truly believe that it will make business, and the corporate world, a better place.

<u>CONTRARIANS WANTED</u>

In a globalised economy like ours, standardisation happens at all levels. From business models and behaviours to shopping habits and lifestyles, it has become very difficult to tell the difference between east and west, and a sort of natural conformity rule seems to have taken hold.

Especially in the business world, being "politically correct" is the preferred attitude to almost every decision.

Better not stir up controversy, right?

Well, I think that the fear of saying something that might – just might – be interpreted in the wrong way has actually turned into a very negative attitude, a sort of hiding technique. Instead, we prefer not to say anything at all.

It can be found in political debates, in public discussions and of course in business situations too.

It's in the small things. It's about replying "that's a great question" to anything anybody asks you, when what you really think is "that's a really dumb one". It's about agreeing with the big boss because he is, after all, the big boss and cannot be wrong.

And it's in bigger things too, for example when a public policy decision, not generally accepted, needs to be made for the "good" of the community.

What really captures my attention is how, I guess, it's easier for many to just swallow whatever a so-called qualified source tells them, across almost any topic or field, on TV shows, newspapers or online media. The rationale for this behaviour is probably that by not exposing their real thoughts or beliefs, people think they are safe. Truth is, they are not.

I think that practicing disbelief should be encouraged at all levels. Pupils should not believe what they are told by teachers, TV viewers should beware of the news, governments should definitely never be believed (but I guess that's an easy thing to do!).

The point is not to ignore all those sources, but rather it's about learning more on your own terms, and then taking another look. Take a stand and fight if it can't be helped.

Thanks to the internet and the WWW, it's easier than ever to document yourself and build your own point of view. Plenty or resources, mostly free. All it takes is a little bit of time and some healthy curiosity.

The effect that such a simple recipe can have is to turn us into more balanced, opinionated and fact grounded challengers. A step up from challengers, and we become contrarians.

Sure, contrarians can be seen as troublemakers. But they are also driven individuals.

They can become not very sociable. But they happily break the rules, and can more often than not become the precipitating effect that makes innovation happen.

Two of my favourite contrarians are the late author Michael Crichton and renowned skeptical environmentalist Bjorn Lomborg. The two got entangled a few years ago in an epic discussion with the so-called cognoscenti (led by a publicity-hungry and shamelessly self-promoting former US vice-president Al Gore) on the global warming dispute, and that in effect turned into an ideal platform to showcase contrarian attitude at its best.

That and fostering passionate discussions that have increased public interest and knowledge on both positions. Which after all is the real reason why we need more contrarians.

HOW TO MAKE SOMETHING

As we all know, an idea without execution is little more than a waste of time. Similarly, executing on anything that doesn't have a clear idea behind it (or in which you do not really believe) also represents a waste. So what's the formula to make your ideas into something?

Ideas can come very easy. Big, small, difficult to describe or simple and straightforward. But as we know, ideas without execution really are not worth much.

So how do you move your one-in-a-million business idea into execution phase? You certainly need a strong objective to drive you (to make money can be one, but should not be the only one!). The accepted wisdom is for you to find your passion first, then to build something.

A quest for passion.

Developing your passion strengthens your belief, and if you passionately believe in something you will be in a better position to "make" your idea real.

However, finding your passion might not be as straightforward as it sounds.

Especially for very curious people, who want to try a lot of different things and might find it difficult to choose. Or for those who have a very short attention span, or who get bored very quickly (even of things they like very much...).

If you are one of them, you will need variety to keep you concentrated and sharp on what you do. So for you, a standard routine would be, for example, to "read-write-play guitar-watch a movie-surf the web", sequentially or often simultaneously packed into a very short timeframe. The principle is, it's the variety element that enhances each and every experience, and makes it whole at the same time.

An attention deficit can be a problem of course, especially if you want to embark on an entrepreneurial trajectory. As they say, you need to stick at things to make them happen.

The majority of entrepreneurs, for example, are required to juggle as many balls as they can 24×7, so the ability to quickly shift your focus to different and often unrelated things might actually turn into an asset, and make the transition into execution somewhat less painful.

What is passion anyway?

How would you define passion? Is it to care deeply for something – for a social or political cause for example? Or is it the impulse to learn everything about it that turns it into your passion? And if you're passionate about something, is it healthy to be driven to change it and run the risk of turning it into something that you might not feel that passionate about anymore?

Talk about your passion to anybody who would listen, it's very important to expose it and share it with as large a number of people as possible. They may not know it yet, but they might be as passionate as you are. I believe that this step alone will be the most important one in your quest.

Passion + Ideas + Focus = Making things!

Once you've found your passion, and you've come up with cool ideas, you need to give yourself enough time to focus and "make" those ideas into something tangible, even if it's just a minimum viable product to start with. Starting with an idea before finding your passion can be done, but you will risk wasting way too much time chasing many differently wild propositions. For me, it has to be passion first.

Don't be afraid of making things that break.

So if passion and belief are in place, you're on the right path to "idea making". Practice and iteration will make it easier for you to get going.

Interestingly, if you develop this habit, the idea-making practice will in turn become the fundamental vehicle for your passions! Making stuff transforms the intangible into tangible, truer to others and even to you. The stuff you make becomes the token that gets passed around, that feeds back into the excitement and nurtures your belief.

So feed your ideas with passion, let them blossom and make them happen. And never be afraid of failures: those are only there to make you try harder the next time.

5 PROBLEMS OF MANAGING COMPLEXITY

The main issue with managing complexity of course is that you should not! As already discussed, our aim should be to eliminate complexity in everything we do.

Undeniably, our life has become incredibly busy, and with that also very complex. Technology and modernisation have certainly helped speed up a great number of our daily activities, but only to give us more time to squeeze even more new ones in. It all adds up to complexity, in terms of behaviours, processes and relationships.

In business, the moment you accept to manage high complexity, you're doomed. Here's why.

1. Complexity is a beast that feeds upon itself (or a self-fulfilling prophecy if you will). The more complexity you get used to manage, the more complexity you will end up with. The problem with someone who's very good at managing complexity is that they will always be able to manage more, hence will not really feel the urge or the need to help eliminate it. Don't assume that complexity mainly comes from external factors, in fact it mostly comes from within your company.

2. If you are good at managing complexity, you will not only effortlessly take on more, but you will constantly generate more. Rather than thinking "let's try to make my point in three slides rather than thirty" you will go "it wasn't too difficult for me

to develop fifty slides, so maybe I can just add a few to provide more background information". You revel in your complex world, you feel empowered and that power goes to your head. By the time you cycle through this a few times, you will not really feel much difference, but your colleagues and your audience in general will. You will drive everybody else crazy, and your company too.

3. To be short, concise and simple is a hell lot more difficult than to be long, verbose and complex. Blaise Pascal (1623-1662), French philosopher and mathematician, famously once wrote to a friend "*Apologies for sending you this long letter, I just did not have the time to write you a short one*". He was right of course. It's much easier to be long and convoluted, hence complex, than short, sharp, direct and to the point. Any blogger or writer knows this very well. Unfortunately, business managers and leaders don't necessarily know.

4. Complexity is darn expensive. Compute the time that you spend on average trying to make sense of any business material. Or product brochure. Or even email. Add to that the time spent in meetings where most of the discussion is around the interpretation of some data points, or reports. All money that could be better spent somewhere else. Huge expense caused by pervasive complexity.

5. The "if you cannot convince them, confuse them" syndrome. This is very common in business. It's the behaviour adopted by someone unable to get his point through.

Seeing you staring in a vacuum, he decides to add even more complexity to his formula. The principle is that if he's not able to make you understand his pitch, then he can at least fill your head with confusion and doubt. Complexity as a smokescreen and a declaration of superiority. You should feel at least a little guilty for not being able to understand and digest complexity like him. This is also known as "pitching by bullshitting", a practice very, very common in most business environments, at all levels (arguably, the closer you get to the top, the more of it you get...).

So if you are good at managing complexity, stop now.

Maybe you don't realize it, but you are turning from an asset to a liability very quickly.

You are using complexity to resist change, most probably as a cheap device to hide things, or to murk them at a minimum. Not to mention the fact that you will eventually choke your organization.

In a way, you're behaving like those IT managers resisting outsourcing for fear of ending up out of a job.

Carry on like that, and you will be the next one in line to be fired. You've been warned...

CAN YOU SEE THE BIG PICTURE?

More than ever the business world requires clarity of strategic directions and vision for companies and enterprises to thrive and grow.

A vision, that in my view, does not necessarily have to be provided from the top, but that can be built at all company's levels, and that you can lead to make happen.

To be able to build a vision, we need to become better at looking at the big picture. Which fundamentally means being able to understand the elementary blocks, how they are related to each other, the cause-effect dynamics, the internal and external influencing factors. I like to define all of those elements as "quantitative".

There are other "qualitative" factors that need to be taken into account to build the big picture. Things like the projection of the market dynamics, the forecasting of the technological trends, the anticipation of changing commercial terms, etc.

The balancing act of charting quantitative and qualitative factors will help you build a better vision.

In terms of quantitative data, try to avoid what I call the "completeness syndrome". A lot of colleagues I've worked with find impossible to start any given project without a full set of data, or in other words they can only work by starting with the details. In fact, they become obsessed with content.

Others focus too much on details: numbers, rates, statistics, customer feedbacks, all thrown together.

My learning is that instead of focusing on completeness and details - or content - we should focus on context.

I believe that context is how we human beings make sense of the world. If you have clarity on setting a given context, than everything else will fall into the right place. More content can always be found, but it will be meaningless if it's not projected against the right backdrop.

Context and relation between things are what really provide value.

Maria Montessori, an Italian physician and educator best known for the philosophy of education, famously remarked at the beginning of the twentieth century that *"to teach the details means to bring confusion, to establish the relation between things means bringing knowledge"*.

It sounds very relevant to business too.

ABOUT THE AUTHOR

With studies in electronics engineering, computer science and marketing, Gianni's professional trajectory developed through jobs at Olivetti, Italia Online, Yahoo! and Hewlett-Packard, mainly with international responsibilities and roles across IT services, business management, e-commerce, sales and marketing. A curious reader, passionate writer and blogger, he's currently based in Italy near Milan. When not working, he plays guitar in a blues band, enjoys traveling with his family and loves reading, sports and photography.
"Leader$hip - an insider guide" is his first book.

Follow: http://twitter.com/giannianchois

Connect: it.linkedin.com/in/giannianchois

http://leadershipthebook.weebly.com

leadershipthebook@gmail.com

www.ingramcontent.com/pod-product-compliance
Lightning Source LLC
Chambersburg PA
CBHW070857180526
45168CB00005B/1851